France, German
the Western Alli

D1439908

The New Europe: Interdisciplinary Perspectives
Stanley Hoffman, Series Editor

France, Germany, and the Western Alliance
  Philip H. Gordon

The European Sisyphus: Essays on Europe, 1964–1994
  Stanley Hoffmann

FORTHCOMING

The European Union: Politics and Policies
  John Spencer McCormick

Integrating Social Europe: The International Construction
  of a Democratic Polity   *Wolfgang Streeck*

France, Germany, and the Western Alliance

Philip H. Gordon

Westview Press

BOULDER • SAN FRANCISCO • OXFORD

The New Europe: Interdisciplinary Perspectives

Copyright © 1995 by Westview Press, Inc.

Published in 1995 in the United States of America by Westview Press, Inc., 5500 Central Avenue, Boulder, Colorado 80301-2877, and in the United Kingdom by Westview Press, 36 Lonsdale Road, Summertown, Oxford OX2 7EW

A CIP catalog record for this book is available from the Library of Congress.
ISBN 0-8133-2555-2—ISBN 0-8133-2554-4 (pbk.)

Printed and bound in the United States of America

The paper used in this publication meets the requirements
of the American National Standard for Permanence of Paper
for Printed Library Materials Z39.48-1984.

10   9   8   7   6   5   4   3   2   1

For Rachel, Noah, and Ben

Contents

Preface   3
Acknowledgments   7

1 Franco-German Security Cooperation, 1949-1989   9

Contrasting Strategic Cultures Since World War II   9
Cooperation from the 1950s to the 1970s   12
The Relaunching of Franco-German Cooperation in the 1980s   17
Adapting to Gorbachev   22
Notes   24

**2 The Franco-German Partnership and the Western Alliance,
     1989-1994   31**

Post-Cold War Challenges to the Franco-German Partnership   31
The National Lessons of the Persian Gulf War   35
Institutions: The Debate About the Eurocorps   40
Ensuring Security and Stability in Eastern Europe   46
War and Diplomacy in Former Yugoslavia   53
Notes   66

**3 Post-Cold War Trends in French and German Security
     Policies   83**

France   83
Germany   89
Notes   93

**4 Conclusions: The Franco-German Partnership and the
     Western Alliance   101**

Notes   108

Selected Bibliography   109
Index   121
About the Book and Author   128

Preface

The thirtieth anniversary of the 1963 Elysée Treaty of Friendship and Coopera-tion between France and Germany gave leaders in the two countries the oppor-tunity to celebrate the most successful example of bilateral reconciliation the world has ever known. "Hereditary enemies" that had fought three catastrophic wars between 1870 and 1945, France and Germany began in the early 1950s to accept one another as partners, codified that partnership under Charles de Gaulle and Konrad Adenauer in the 1963 treaty, and for the next thirty years went on to build a relationship so intimate that it became customary to refer to it in mari-tal—rather than martial—terms. The triumph of the reconciliation was that France and Germany not only overcame their hostile past and agreed on a "peace-ful coexistence" but that the two countries actually formed a strategic partner-ship seen, correctly, as no less than an "alliance within the alliance."[1]

France and Germany's partners, however, have always viewed the Paris-Bonn couple with a certain ambivalence. On one hand, the allies were re-lieved to see the profound reconciliation of Western Europe's two biggest states, and the Americans, in particular, appreciated the idea that France and Germany could assume some of the burdens of Western defense. On the other hand, however, most of France and Germany's allies have always been con-cerned that "bilateralism" or "sub-structures" within the alliance would under-mine its common tasks. For the smaller states in Europe, the Franco-German condominium could produce the same kind of hegemony within Europe that French leaders said they were trying to avoid from Washington and could set an unhealthy precedent for bilateralism and faits accomplis. For the United States, Franco-German security cooperation has often seemed a plan to marginalize American leadership and to free Europe from its military depend-ence on, and thereby its political subordination to, the United States.

This study analyzes the Franco-German security partnership in the post-Cold War era and its implications for the Western alliance. Intended for read-ers on both sides of the Atlantic, it examines not only the content and pros-pects of Franco-German security cooperation in the post-Cold War era but also the potential advantages and perils of that bilateral cooperation for the European Union, NATO, and individual Western states. The study also identi-

3

fies new national security policy trends in France and Germany and considers their implications for the West. It is my hope that the book will be of interest both to students—for whom I have included an historical overview—and to specialized observers of European affairs, who, like myself, have been trying to figure out whether France and Germany can really pursue common security policies in the post-Cold War world, and what their success or failure to do so means for the United States and their other allies.

The future of the Franco-German security partnership is important not only for the French and the Germans themselves but for the rest of Europe and the United States. For Europe, agreement between Paris and Bonn is the key to any potential "common foreign and security policy" and—as subsequent chapters will show—there is little chance of coherent European policy when France and Germany do not manage to coordinate their analyses, policies, and means. For the United States, Franco-German cooperation can provide the leadership of the "European pillar" that Americans have always professed to support and, thereby, help to reduce some of the international duties and costs for the United States at a time when American resources are increasingly limited. If mismanaged, however, Franco-German security cooperation could create divisions within the European Union and drive the United States out of a European role—without leaving anything dependable or effective in its place.

This book is divided into four parts. Chapter 1 examines the development of Franco-German security cooperation since World War II and addresses the question of "strategic culture" in the two countries. It argues that although the development of the partnership over those four decades was truly remarkable, France and Germany never really managed to develop common views and perspectives on the most basic issues of national security, the use of military force, and alliance relations. Postwar Franco-German security cooperation was thus a product of the Cold War; this does not necessarily mean that the partnership will wither, but it does mean that its resilience under the present circumstances is untested.

Chapter 2 places the Franco-German partnership in its new context and argues that the challenges of the post-Cold War world will be greater than those faced during the Cold War. With the Soviet threat gone, Germany unified, the American role in Europe uncertain, and great potential for instability to Europe's east and south, Franco-German cooperation will be more difficult and less natural than in the past. The chapter also examines four important aspects of the France-Germany-Atlantic Alliance security relationship since 1989—the Persian Gulf War, the debates over the Eurocorps, policies toward Eastern Europe (and the former Soviet Union), and the war in former Yugoslavia. The analysis demonstrates an ongoing and determined effort in Paris and Bonn to coordinate and integrate their security policies but a persistent inability to reach truly common positions or to build adequate means to implement them. These case studies also provide evidence that France and Germany are as likely to share security policy positions with other Western allies as they are with each other.

Chapter 3 identifies and discusses new trends in French and German security policies since 1989. These include, for France, a more cooperative attitude toward the United States and NATO, a continued desire to play a prominent global security role, and a growing preoccupation with Germany. In Germany, the trends include continued support for the United States and NATO, a growing (but still highly circumscribed) willingness to play an international security role, and a declining relative interest in France. From an alliance perspective, the trends in both countries have both positive and negative elements; they suggest the possibility for much improved cooperation and burden-sharing within NATO, for example, but could also lead to divergence in French, German, and other allied interests and perceptions.

Finally, the study's conclusion looks at the future of the Franco-German security partnership and its consequences for the European Union and Atlantic Alliance. It shows that the general commitment in Paris and Bonn to Franco-German security cooperation is still strong and that the principle of continued cooperation is not in doubt. But the analysis also suggests that a truly common and effective Franco-German security policy is unlikely; the national interests and perceptions of the two countries are not only still different, but they are probably more different today than during the Cold War. Consequently, the conclusion also argues that American and European fears of Franco-German bilateralism undermining the broader Western alliances are exaggerated, and that the allies have more to gain than to lose from the Franco-German pursuit of their special relationship. The problem for the West is not so much that France and Germany have formed a cohesive political-military force within Europe but that they have failed to do so.

Notes

[1] See Robert Picht, ed., *Das Bündnis im Bündnis: Deutsch-französiche Beziehungen im internationalen Spannungsfeld* (Berlin: Severin und Siedler, 1982); and also David Haglund, *Alliance Within the Alliance?: Franco-German Military Cooperation and the European Pillar of Defense* (Boulder, CO: Westview, 1991).

Acknowledgments

Most of the research for this book was undertaken during 1992-1993 while I was a guest scholar at the Deutsche Gesellschaft für Auswärtige Politik (DGAP) in Bonn, where my research—and my existence—was generously sponsored by the German Marshall Fund of the United States. I also benefited greatly while in Bonn from participation in the Bundeskanzler-Scholarship program and am grateful to the Chancellor's office and the Alexander von Humboldt Foundation for their help and support. I updated and expanded the study during 1993-1994 while an assistant professor at the Johns Hopkins University's Paul H. Nitze School of Advanced International Studies (SAIS) in Washington DC; one could hardly ask for a more stimulating or well-situated place to study the implications of European foreign policies on the United States. Needless to say, I am also grateful to the many officials in Paris, Bonn, and Washington who took time out of their schedules to talk with me; I hope they will find their views accurately—if mostly anonymously—reflected in this book.

An earlier, shorter version of this study was published in German as *Die Deutsch-Französische Partnerschaft und die Atlantische Allianz* (Bonn: Forschungsinstitut der Deutschen Gesellschaft für Auswärtige Politik, April 1994), Arbeitspapiere zur Internationalen Politik no. 82. The DGAP was an exceptional place to study German politics and foreign affairs during a year when Germany was trying to figure out what role it was to play in the world, and I thank then-codirector Hanns Maull for encouraging me to write this study and Director Karl Kaiser for providing the superb environment in which to do it. The German edition of this study does not contain the historical background included here as Chapter 2; for parts of that I drew on a chapter I published earlier in a book edited by Patrick McCarthy, *France-Germany 1983-93: The Struggle to Cooperate* (New York: St. Martin's Press, 1993). I thank St. Martin's for permission to use parts of that publication here. At SAIS, Rosa Alonso was a good-spirited and over-qualified research assistant, and in London Juliet Sampson patiently and carefully saw the book through its final stages. Clare Wilkes put everything together without hitches, and Susan McEachern of Westview Press was an expert editor and a delight to work with.

Personal acknowledgments always come last but they are never least. My wife, Rachel, put up with the usual bad moods associated with writing and even allowed me to take some trips to Paris without her. Noah, born (like the Eurocorps) in the spring of 1992, was thoughtful enough to make sure his father was up early every morning so that no excessive research time was wasted on frivolous things like sleep. His brother Benjamin was born just as these galleys were being completed. This book is dedicated to the three of them.

Philip H. Gordon

1

Franco-German Security Cooperation, 1949-1989

Contrasting Strategic Cultures Since World War II

All countries have what might be called a national strategic culture, a set of attitudes and policies toward defense and security that arises from history, geography, and political culture.[1] Although France and West Germany obviously shared a preoccupation with the overriding Western security concern of the postwar era—the Soviet threat—the two countries had very distinct perspectives and priorities within that overarching consensus. Paris and Bonn agreed that Western Europe had to be defended and that cooperation between the two countries, within the context of an Atlantic Alliance, was a critical element in that defense. Yet at both the public and elite levels, French and German attitudes toward security and defense were highly divergent.

For France, the overriding foreign policy goal after World War II was the restoration of French status as a great—or at least significant—power, including in the military domain. This was not, as is sometimes suggested, a uniquely Gaullist ambition that emerged in the 1960s, but one that was present from the very start of the postwar era. Humiliated by their sudden and shocking defeat in June 1940, French leaders set out quickly to recover their lost status and prestige by insisting on a French occupation zone in Germany, demanding a seat on the United Nations Security Council, and seeking to reestablish French colonial possessions around the globe. When General de Gaulle came back to power in 1958, he made the pursuit of grandeur the cornerstone of his foreign policy and built an independent nuclear force to support France's claim to great power status.[2] None of his successors abandoned this aim, and throughout the 1970s and 1980s, maintaining and augmenting France's status and rank was a primary element of French strategic culture.[3]

West Germany's postwar foreign policy goals were both more modest and more parochial. Not only did defeat and occupation prevent the Germans from seeking a prominent postwar military role, but the experience of the war, and the guilt it engendered, also seemed to sap from the Germans any will to do so. Rather than seek prestige through the reestablishment of its military might and international responsibilities, West Germany's postwar leaders sought to avoid a prominent world role and to concentrate on domestic and economic objectives. Although its economy and population soon became greater than those of France (or the United Kingdom), the postwar Federal Republic was neither a member of the United Nations Security Council nor a nuclear power, and it did not play any global military role. Unlike France, West Germany did not seek to display its power proudly and prominently but, rather, went out of its way to play it down or cover it up.[4]

A second fundamental element of postwar France's strategic culture that differed from the Federal Republic's was the pursuit of national military independence. Again, not only for Charles de Gaulle but for his predecessors and successors, maximizing French autonomy was an overriding political and military goal. French leaders who had lived through World War II had seen the consequences of France's reliance on the "Anglo-Saxons" for security, and many had resolved never to be so dependent on others again. De Gaulle, who was obsessed with independence, insisted on the total autonomy of the French nuclear force and in 1966 withdrew France from NATO's integrated military commands. While the policy of independence was always implemented pragmatically, and France never had any intention of trying to "go it alone," even its most cooperative leaders—Valéry Giscard d'Estaing and François Mitterrand—were careful to uphold this aspect of the Gaullist legacy. Even as the 1980s came to an end, France still chose to remain outside NATO integration, refused to discuss publicly any coordination of its nuclear force, and produced more than 95 percent of its military equipment at home.

The attitude toward military independence in postwar West Germany was quite different. After World War II, the Federal Republic was not only militarily "dependent," but in fact did not exist as a country until 1949 and had no army until 1955. Once the Cold War began, West Germany—severed from its eastern half, nonnuclear, and on the border of a Soviet empire occupied by the huge Red Army—had no choice but to rely heavily on the support of its western allies, and in particular on the United States. Whereas France, with no direct dispute with the Soviets and inevitably protected by the Allied forces in Germany, had the "luxury" of trumpeting its independence from Washington, the Federal Republic was condemned to accept its interdependence or even outright dependence. The tragic legacy of German unilateralism from the 1870s to 1945, moreover, prohibited the Germans from acting alone, especially where military affairs were concerned. West Germany's strategic culture thus emphasized cooperation, multilateralism, and integration— not independence, like France's.

Finally, postwar France and West Germany had very different attitudes about military force. Each country drew very different lessons from the war itself. France's precipitous defeat taught it never again to be caught unprepared militarily, and its ultimate achievement of victor status produced the obvious message that it was better to be on the winning side in a war. Germans, on the other hand, learned of the dangers of possessing an excess of military might and felt most directly the tragedy of what military conflict on one's own territory can bring. Whereas postwar France thus associated military force with victory, independence, power, and glory, West Germany associated it with defeat, dependence, ignominy, and disaster. What was true of military forces in general was all the more true of nuclear forces: For France, these ultimate weapons were symbols of the country's security, independence, and technical prowess, whereas in Germany—the potential battleground for a European nuclear war—they were constantly present reminders of the horrific fate that awaited them if war ever broke out.[5]

To put it baldly, then (and describing national strategic cultures briefly always requires some simplification), Franco-German military cooperation in the postwar period seems to have taken place despite important differences in perspective between the two countries, not because of a fundamental rapprochement of views. What France sought in the security domain, Germany often shunned. What France pursued with vigor, Germany largely avoided. What France was allowed or got away with, Germany was prohibited or did not want.

Cooperation from the 1950s to the 1970s

Despite these very different postwar strategic cultures, Franco-German co-operation advanced steadily, if intermittently, during the postwar era.[6] France and Germany may once have been enemies and may have drawn different conclusions from their respective histories, but they both realized that bilateral security cooperation after World War II would be essential—in different ways—to their national fates. Already by the end of the war, in fact, even nationalists like Charles de Gaulle had a sense that France and Germany would have to join forces in the new geopolitics of the postwar world; de Gaulle's early vision was of a French-led partnership with a decentralized and truncated Germany, but it was a vision of cooperation, nonetheless.[7]

The first attempt at Franco-German security cooperation, of course, was a spectacular failure. In October 1950, with the United States calling for German rearmament following the outbreak of the Korean War, French prime minister René Pleven proposed a European Defense Community (EDC) that would integrate French and German military forces into a common European army. In Pleven's original formulation, the EDC would be a fully integrated European force of small national units under the responsibility of a European defense minister and overseen by an assembly on the model of the European Coal and Steel Community that was being set up at the same time.[8] German chancellor Konrad Adenauer, keen on rehabilitating his country on the basis of equality and European integration, saw in the EDC an opportunity to do so and became a strong supporter.[9] The Pleven plan was finally signed in 1952 in the form of a watered-down treaty (the European defense minister had been dropped and the integrated military units were larger than originally planned), but two years later, after vigorous and divisive debate in France, it was rejected by the French parliament, which opposed the very equality the Germans sought. The Communists (and others) in France could not bear to see a Germany with national military forces, and the Gaullists (and others) could not bear to see a France without them.[10] The lesson of the EDC episode was that France, at least, was not yet ready for security partnership with its former enemy from the east.[11]

The EDC was quickly replaced by a compromise solution that, in 1955, saw Germany obtain national military forces (ironically, the very thing the French had tried to forestall with the EDC) that would be integrated into the Western European Union (WEU) and NATO. In this sense, France and Germany had technically become security partners. But an American-dominated NATO was by no means a Franco-German affair, and the WEU (which in any event had largely been supplanted by NATO's creation in 1949), became little more than a European forum to control German rearmament.[12] Franco-German political and economic cooperation was, of course, proceeding apace, but the 1957 Treaty of Rome that founded the European Economic Community (EEC) studiously avoided inclusion of military matters.

The late 1950s did see advances in Franco-German military industrial cooperation, as well as a putative experiment in nuclear cooperation. Between January 1957 and May 1958, German defense minister Franz-Josef Strauss met on numerous occasions with his French counterparts (Maurice Bourgès-Manoury and Jacques Chaban-Delmas) and explored the possibility of France and Germany (along with Italy) together developing nuclear technologies for military use as well as the means of nuclear delivery.[13] The joint nuclear talks, however, never got beyond the exploratory stage, were not fully supported by the German government or public at large, and were in any case cut off in May 1958. Just as the EDC was more than anything an expedient meant to avoid true German rearmament, the Franco-German nuclear flirtation of the late 1950s was primarily a way for France to take advantage of Bonn's financial and technical resources without allowing it equal control over a nuclear bomb. National interest considerations were—as they would remain—the primary factor driving Franco-German security cooperation.

The coming to power of Charles de Gaulle in France in 1958 gave new impetus to the stagnating Franco-German strategic partnership. De Gaulle shared with Adenauer a certain mistrust of American intentions and reliability as well as a desire to create a West European entity that could stand up—in different ways—to the superpowers of East and West. From their first, friendly meeting at Rambouillet in September 1958 through the signing of the landmark Franco-German cooperation treaty (Elysée Treaty) in January 1963, de Gaulle and Adenauer worked to develop a Franco-German military relationship that would not only mark the reconciliation of the two countries, but would also form the heart of a Europe ultimately capable of asserting itself militarily (and, thereby, diplomatically). Their symbolic reconciliation included Adenauer's July 1962 visit to France (during which he prayed together with de Gaulle at Rheims cathedral) and de Gaulle's triumphant tour of Germany two months later (during which he was swarmed by throngs of Germans appreciative of his support for reconciliation).[14] The symbolism also included the organization and observation of joint Franco-German tank maneuvers on the Mourmelon plains in

France, the first time in history that French and German military forces actually maneuvered together. More concretely, the Elysée Treaty expressed the objectives of a "rapprochement of military doctrines" and "common conceptions" about European defense, and it institutionalized regular meetings between the French and German defense ministers (every three months), French and German chiefs of staff (every two months), and French and German heads of state or government (at least every six months).[15] Far more than anything that took place during the preceding decade, the Elysée Treaty was a sign that proactive Franco-German security cooperation was underway.

Yet it would be wrong to overlook the limits to the partnership even under its great promoters. Although de Gaulle was certainly sincere in his desire for Franco-German cooperation, it was also clear that he intended France to be the leader of a rather unequal relationship. The general's abrupt termination of Franco-German nuclear discussions in 1958, his attempts later that year to organize a tripartite leadership of NATO that would exclude Germany, and his continual insistence on French military independence were all signs that his vision of Franco-German security cooperation might not be exactly what the Germans had in mind.[16] Adenauer was rightfully furious when de Gaulle failed to consult him before rejecting Great Britain's application to the European Economic Community just one week before the Elysée Treaty was to be signed, and while Adenauer went ahead with the treaty nonetheless, German parliamentarians did not. The Bundestag refused to ratify the Franco-German treaty before attaching a preamble stating its unwavering commitments to NATO and to British participation in the EEC, thus undermining the treaty's very essence in the eyes of de Gaulle.[17] Even more damaging, the replacement of Adenauer by the liberal Atlanticist Ludwig Erhard in October 1963 meant that the Franco-German security relationship would be frozen for the foreseeable future. With Adenauer gone, de Gaulle gave up plans to co-opt Germany in his Cold War diplomatic and security strategy, and instead turned to a more independent, nationalist path that allowed him to challenge NATO in the West and pursue détente with the Soviet Union in the East.[18] Erhard, more interested in economics than grand diplomacy or defense in any case, acted to solidify West Germany's Atlantic connections and began very tentative forays of his own into the domain of *Ostpolitik*.[19] The institutional aspects of the Franco-German treaty were largely implemented, and some limited Franco-German arms collaboration in the late 1960s took place; but the spirit of the treaty as envisioned by de Gaulle and Adenauer was dead.

The early 1970s saw another change of leaders but no improvement in security cooperation. Under Chancellor Willy Brandt from 1969 to 1973, Germany was no longer as Atlanticist as it had been under Erhard, and with Georges Pompidou in the Elysée from 1969 to 1974, France was no longer as nationalist as it had been under de Gaulle. But there were new obstacles to replace the old ones. Brandt's overwhelming diplomatic priority was *Ostpolitik*, which meant establishing new relationships with the states of Eastern Europe, not firming up Western defenses against them. From 1970 to 1972 Brandt sought, and obtained, treaty agreements with the Soviet Union, Poland, and East Germany recognizing the Federal Republic's postwar borders and establishing relations with the Eastern bloc states. Brandt's West Germany remained committed to NATO (indeed, a strong Western alliance was an admitted prerequisite for his forays into the East[20]), but Franco-German security cooperation had little role to play in the pursuit of this German national interest.

France's leaders looked at its neighbor's new diplomacy with suspicion and consternation. If the Cold War were coming to an end and Europe's division fading, the Federal Republic would no longer need to be so concerned about maintaining close relations with France. A more confident, assertive, and economically prosperous West Germany, no longer so dependent for security on its Western neighbors and intent on reaching new accords with the East, risked leaving Paris diplomatically isolated and undermining France's own (self-designated) role as the special interlocutor of the Communist half of Europe. Pompidou and Foreign Minister Michel Jobert had been supportive when it was de Gaulle who was breaking paths with his own détente (culminating with his trip to Moscow in June 1966), but when the tables turned they began to fear that Germany was "edging away from Europe."[21] To compensate, France sought to improve its relations with Great Britain, which it finally allowed into the Common Market in 1973. Jobert did seek briefly in 1973 to win German support for a relaunching of the WEU as a means of strengthening European military independence, but he was promptly rebuffed by Bonn.[22] None of this did very much to promote the idea of a special Franco-German security partnership, and it is difficult to find any important initiatives in this area during the tenures of Georges Pompidou and Willy Brandt.[23]

It was, thus, not until the arrival in office of Valéry Giscard d'Estaing in France and Helmut Schmidt in Germany that the Franco-German security partnership would begin to make real progress again. While the main successes of bilateral cooperation under Giscard and Schmidt were in the economic and financial area—most notably the creation of the European Monetary System (EMS)—they were both also committed to enhancing bilateral security cooperation as well. Both leaders were convinced that the European community they wanted to create would never be complete without a strategic dimension.

As France's most Atlanticist and "pro-European" leader of the postwar period, Giscard's willingness to back away from some of the dogmas of Gaullist independence facilitated security cooperation with West Germany. From 1974 to 1976, the new French president made a number of changes in military policy that enhanced France's commitment to West German defense and France's role in European security more generally. In 1975, Giscard reorganized the French army (by raising the number of divisions and making them smaller) in order to enhance mobility and versatility, and he dissolved the old territorial defense system (*défense opérationelle du territoire*) that seemed to imply strictly national concerns. The 1976 five-year military program law confirmed France's new commitment to German and European security by stating that "it would be illusory to hope that France could have any more than reduced sovereignty if her neighbors had been occupied by a hostile power," and later that year Chief of Staff of the Armed Forces General Guy Méry elaborated the military doctrine of enlarged sanctuary (*sanctuarisation élargie*) that seemed to imply a French nuclear cover for the Federal Republic.[24] Finally, Giscard increased French military spending significantly, and after nearly fifteen years of emphasizing nuclear forces, the French military procurement budget began to shift the balance to the conventional forces needed to play a role in European defense. All of these changes effectively eliminated the old French distinction between the "battle for Germany" and the "battle for France."[25]

The arrival in Bonn of Helmut Schmidt facilitated Franco-German security cooperation no less than the arrival of Giscard. Whereas Brandt, a former mayor of Berlin, and his diplomatic adviser, Egon Bahr, were visionary politicians with sentimental and personal bonds to the East, Schmidt was a pragmatic Atlanticist who had spent most of his political career dealing intimately (as defense and finance minister) with the Atlantic Alliance and Western Europe. Most of the main goals of *Ostpolitik*, in any case, were already achieved by the end of 1972, and it would have been difficult for Schmidt to pursue further achievements in the East without raising excessive suspicions in Washington, Paris, London, and Moscow. Although an Atlanticist on defense issues, Schmidt's interest in promoting an integrated Europe, his sense of increasing German power and responsibility, and most of all his growing skepticism about the reliability of American leadership under Jimmy Carter (fueled by Carter's 1978 sudden cancellation of the neutron bomb that Schmidt had promised to deploy at great political risk) led him to the view that it was time for Europe to assert itself more diplomatically. This meant more than anything the reinvigoration of Franco-German cooperation, and Schmidt welcomed his friend Giscard's mutual willingness to expand cooperation in all areas.

But even under the committed leadership of Giscard and Schmidt there were clear limits to Franco-German security cooperation, and those limits were soon reached. The far-reaching changes Giscard began in 1974 were soon beaten back by French conservatives of the right and left who feared the president was selling out France's hard-fought independence. After Prime Minister Jacques Chirac was replaced in 1976 by Raymond Barre—whose mission it was to concentrate on economic affairs after the oil crisis—the doctrinal and military innovations of 1974 to 1976 came to a halt. Schmidt remained prepared to carry on with bilateral security cooperation but was disappointed when Giscard failed to support him on the most important security issue of the 1970s for the Federal Republic—the deployment of NATO's intermediate-range nuclear forces (INF), decided in December 1979. Giscard took no official position on the missile deployment on the grounds that France was not concerned by NATO's nuclear decisions (the real reasons were that he was afraid of accusations of "Atlanticism" and that he did not want to give the Soviets a pretext for including French warheads in arms control negotiations) and thus left it to Schmidt to fight what turned out to be a losing political battle within his party. When Cold War tensions heated up again with the Soviet invasion of Afghanistan in late 1979 and the military crackdown in Poland in 1981, the Germans were reminded that their most important security partner remained the United States, and the Franco-German partnership again took a back seat. Schmidt recounts in his memoirs that he and Giscard had made far-reaching plans to relaunch the security partnership at the start of the 1980s, but fate—in the form of domestic politics—intervened: By the end of 1982 both leaders were out of office.[26]

The Relaunching of Franco-German Cooperation in the 1980s

To the surprise of many, the changes of government that took place in Paris and Bonn in 1981 and 1982 did not derail the Franco-German partnership; in fact they may have been prerequisites for its continuation. The French and German socialist parties were moving in opposite directions on security questions at the end of the 1970s; the French Socialist Party (PS) was rallying to nuclear deterrence and the Atlantic Alliance, while the German Social Democratic Party (SPD) was joining the anti-nuclear camp and abandoning the pro-defense Schmidt. Thus it was only the arrival of the socialist Mitterrand (now a strong supporter of the Atlantic Alliance, the French nuclear force, and a hard-line policy toward the Soviet Union) and the conservative Helmut Kohl (similarly firm on NATO, nuclear deterrence, and the USSR) that brought about a convergence of French and German views and made a convergence of their policies possible.

Mitterrand and Kohl wasted little time and in October 1982 devoted their first bilateral meeting to military questions.[27] Although the French president reasserted France's independence and refused German participation in French nuclear planning (perennial French prerequisites), and the German chancellor reaffirmed the Federal Republic's primary tie to NATO and the United States (perennial German prerequisites), the meeting produced some significant results, including the commitment to implement the long-dormant defense clauses of the Elysée Treaty. To expedite the treaty's implementation, the two leaders also decided to create a Franco-German commission on security and defense that would seek to institutionalize the exchange of views between the German and the French on security policy. Not only would defense and foreign ministers of the two countries meet at least twice per year, but the Commission's three specialized working groups—on arms collaboration, military cooperation, and political-strategic issues—would meet even more often, in small groups just below the ministerial level.[28] The success of the treaty's revival should not be exaggerated, but the fact that French and German officials at all levels were now meeting regularly to discuss security—and that they finally managed to reverse the dismal record of military-industrial cooperation during the 1970s by agreeing on the coproduction of a combat helicopter—did lend a certain amount of new momentum to the relationship.[29]

At the start of the following year an even more powerful expression of Franco-German solidarity took place. To celebrate the twentieth anniversary of the Elysée Treaty, Mitterrand traveled to Bonn to make a historic speech before the Bundestag. Breaking with Giscard's ambiguity on the Euromissile (INF) issue, Mitterrand called on the Germans to support deployment of the Pershing missiles and denounced those who wanted to "decouple" Europe from the United States. The speech was not only an effort to ensure the reelection of Mitterrand's partner Kohl but an eloquent personal plea for Franco-German cooperation and peace after generations of war.[30]

Like many other examples of France's commitment to the Franco-German relationship, however, the Bundestag speech was ambiguous. As German observers did not fail to point out, it was rather easy for Mitterrand to call on the Germans to accept the missiles while France, of course, refused to do so itself. Bonn may have been pleased to see France supporting NATO policy and backing a highly controversial deployment but German leaders did not fail to notice that Mitterrand was calling on them to take all the political heat. Still, the Bundestag speech turned out to be a boon to future bilateral cooperation; even ambiguous French support for German policy was better than no support at all, and Helmut Kohl—the eventual winner in the March 1983 Bundestag elections—was grateful for the political boost.

By 1984, the momentum of the Franco-German partnership was strong enough for another attempt at relaunching the Western European Union, the attempted renovation of which had failed ten years earlier because of German suspicions of French motives. This time, however, with the French showing increased interest in European cooperation (and having ceased to portray such cooperation as a means to undermine NATO) and with the Germans themselves coming to believe more sincerely in the need for a "European pillar," the proponents of the WEU were able to give it new life. After France pushed to have the remaining restrictions on German conventional armaments removed from the original WEU treaty, Germany agreed to reactivate the organization.[31]

Even more important to Franco-German defense cooperation than these diplomatic acts were the changes made in French conventional force structures, including, most importantly, the creation of a 47,000-strong *Force d'Action Rapide* (FAR) designed to intervene quickly in Central Europe. In many ways a microcosm of the French attitude toward German security in the postwar era, the FAR was a classic example of France's desire to show concrete interest in European solidarity while holding on to the pretense as well as the reality of national autonomy. On one hand, the FAR was a major sign of growing French support for Germany that would, in the words of French defense minister Charles Hernu, "permit [us], infinitely better than today, to commit ourselves at the side of our allies."[32] At the same time, however, the French commitment to defend West Germany remained ambiguous. French leaders continued to assert that the French government's autonomy was "complete" and that the FAR's independence from NATO structures was "total"; it was unclear whether the FAR would really be capable of playing an important military role.[33] Because the force was designed to intervene in conflicts not only in Europe but overseas (where fighting conditions would be very different), many military experts wondered whether this lightly armed, untested, and extremely heterogeneous force could have much of an impact even if French leaders were prepared to send it to the front.

During the mid-1980s, as leaders in both Paris and Bonn began to doubt American reliability and fear U.S.-Soviet "collusion," Franco-German military cooperation increased commensurately. The Strategic Defense Initiative (which undermined deterrence and drew scarce funds away from European defense), swollen U.S. budget deficits (which put pressure on Washington to reduce defense spending), the October 1986 Reykjavik summit (where Ronald Reagan appeared willing to bargain away Europe's nuclear guarantee), and the 1987 INF treaty (which raised fears of decoupling) all contributed to a sense in Europe that the longstanding American guarantee of European security would have to be supplemented, or perhaps one day even replaced. As French defense minister André Giraud warned at the time, "American consciousness about the problem of European security might not always be so acute."[34] Even in traditionally Atlanticist Germany, security experts had begun to wonder about the long-term American commitment and to call on Europe to take on a greater and more autonomous military role.[35]

Mitterrand and Kohl responded to this situation by moving ever further down the road toward European—and more specifically, Franco-German— defense. In February 1986, the two leaders met (for no less than the twelfth time since the beginning of the previous year) and announced studies on the use of the FAR in Germany, future joint military maneuvers, a telephone crisis "hotline" between Paris and Bonn, and a French commitment—albeit a qualified one—to consult with the Germans before using tactical nuclear weapons in Germany.[36] The military maneuvers planned at this time took place in September of the following year and would prove to be the largest and most significant ever between the two countries. In Operation Bold Sparrow, 20,000 French troops, operating for the first time under German command, joined 55,000 German soldiers deep in the territory of the Federal Republic (in Bavaria and Baden-Wurtenburg, well outside the normal French zone of operation). The operation was not without technical and logistical hitches—French helicopters, for example, arrived late to their designated point of intervention—but the maneuver did show that France was serious about contributing to forward defense and that the FAR could indeed have a role in Central Europe. The maneuvers were also significant for Germany, which agreed (albeit reluctantly) to French demands that Bold

Sparrow take place outside of the NATO structure. This was a Franco-German exercise; NATO's Supreme Allied Commander Europe (SACEUR) was not invited.

By 1986, Franco-German security relations were as good as they had ever been, and the Germans were not unhappy to see changes taking place in Paris. Germany was not given a formal say in French nuclear policy, but the issue was at least confronted and discussed; the French nuclear force was not extended to German territory as some Germans might have hoped, but that force was expanded and made more credible; France's interest in a more autonomous European defense distinct from the Atlantic Alliance that the Germans preferred was not abandoned, but it was no longer presented as an alternative to NATO; French conventional forces were not built up to the levels the Germans might have liked, but they were better organized for participation in Europe; and the French commitment to intervene on the central front with those forces was not made automatic but it was given more substance.

Yet for all this, there were still many problems in the Franco-German military relationship. First, it must be remembered that one of the main catalysts on the French side of the relationship was the suspicion of German intentions (French leaders were concerned about the emergent pacifism of the SPD and the German Green Party)—not the best grounds on which to build a close and enduring relationship. Second, France and Germany continued to have different views about nuclear weapons and about armed forces in general, with Germany still much less comfortable with military power than France. Third, as long as Germany was divided, different French and German attitudes toward the Soviet Union were inevitable: Whereas France had no territorial or minority rights disputes with the Soviet bloc and no major role to play in the East-West military confrontation, Germany had vital national interests—such as *Ostpolitik*—at stake. France had become a status quo power while Germany retained an underlying interest in change. Fourth, despite the increased Paris-Bonn dialogue and frequent high-level meetings, a number of conflicting perspectives remained. To the French, Bonn was still seen as more interested in East Germany, *Ostpolitik*, and the United States than in France (which was probably accurate), and to the Germans, the French seemed to remain more concerned with their national independence and international prestige than with Franco-German relations (which was probably true). Finally, one of the greatest lingering problems of all was that whereas the French believed they had made great strides toward a full commitment to German and European defense—and congratulated themselves for their efforts—the Germans saw how much farther the French had yet to go. Many in the Federal Republic found France's European defense policies under Mitterrand long on symbolism but woefully short on substance—*mehr Schein als Sein* as some Germans liked to say.[37]

Adapting to Gorbachev

Toward the end of the 1980s—at least after 1987—the Franco-German security relationship took on a new character. As the reforms of Soviet leader Mikhail Gorbachev began to appear more and more credible, the most visible impetus to Franco-German defense cooperation of the past thirty years— the Soviet threat—began to fade. Germany, because its stake in détente was by far the greatest, was probably the first country to "take Gorbachev at his word" (as Foreign Minister Hans-Dietrich Genscher requested), and the Germans were the first to welcome the Soviet leader's "new thinking" in foreign policy.[38] By 1988, nearly 60 percent of Germans surveyed had a favorable opinion of the Soviet Union (compared to less than 10 percent in 1981), and by 1989 more Germans trusted Gorbachev than they did any Western leader with the exception of German head of state Richard von Weizsäcker.[39] Just as the Germans had cheered de Gaulle and John F. Kennedy when those leaders visited the Federal Republic in the early 1960s, they now enthusiastically welcomed the Soviet leader, who made a triumphant visit to West Germany in June 1989.

In this sort of climate, progress in the Franco-German security partnership no longer consisted primarily of French efforts to augment their commitment to forward defense or to nuclear deterrence, as it had in the past. Instead, as Germany sought to take advantage of change in Moscow to pursue disarmament and détente, Franco-German cooperation meant most of all French solidarity with Bonn's new security policy stance. Nobody perceived this shift better than François Mitterrand (who in the late 1970s had similarly perceived and taken political advantage of the move away from détente), and a different kind of Franco-German security cooperation began to thrive. Already in early 1987, overcoming widespread reservations in France about the INF treaty that would eliminate the Euromissiles (and possibly raise questions about France's own mid-range nuclear missiles), Mitterrand went along with the wishes of the German government and public opinion and backed the agreement. Similarly, in contrast to Gaullist Prime Minister Jacques Chirac, who in 1988 opposed a further treaty banning short-range nuclear forces (dubbed by some Germans as "German-range nuclear weapons" because they could not reach beyond East or West German targets), Mitterrand supported such a ban and backed Kohl and Foreign Minister Hans Dietrich Genscher at NATO's Brussels summit in March 1988.[40] Finally, Mitterrand also went out of his way before and after his 1988 reelection to stress that French nuclear policy was a policy of deterrence and "non-war," and that France's "final nuclear warning" would not be delivered on German territory.[41] The French president understood, for the time being, at least—better than his conservative partners in the cohabitation government and better than the British and American leaders as well—the critical importance of showing his trust in Bonn.[42]

With French support for Germany's priorities of disarmament and détente made clear and a major potential obstacle to Franco-German cooperation thereby removed, the bilateral relationship could be pursued. On January 22, 1988, Mitterrand and Kohl celebrated the twenty-fifth anniversary of the Elysée Treaty with the creation of a Franco-German defense and security council that would build on the success of the 1982 Commission on Security and Defense. The council, to meet twice per year, would consist of the French president and German chancellor as well as the two countries' foreign ministers, defense ministers, and (ex-officio) the general inspector of the Bundeswehr and the chief of staff of the French armed forces. The council would have at its disposal a council committee, a permanent secretariat (to be located in Paris and initially headed by a German general), and the already existing Commission on Security and Defense.[43] Franco-German cooperation at the end of the decade was also manifested in a historic military exercise in Champagne during September 1989 when 5,000 German soldiers maneuvered with 25,000 French soldiers on the World War I battlefield of the Marne. Added to this was the October 1990 creation of a 4,200-member Franco-German brigade. First proposed by Chancellor Kohl in 1987, the joint brigade was insignificant militarily but was a powerful symbol of cooperation and reconciliation between the two former enemy armies as well as a testing ground for future forms of bilateral military integration.[44]

Thus, on the eve of the revolutions that were about to change fundamentally the basic European security situation that had existed for more than forty years, Franco-German military cooperation was perhaps at its peak. Despite their historic enmity and markedly different strategic cultures, France and Germany had by the end of the 1980s managed to extend their military and security cooperation to levels and areas that were unimaginable forty or even twenty years before. Yet however impressive this special security partnership was, one could not but notice what was still missing. The tiny—and problematic—joint brigade was no more than a fine symbol, and it was already clear by 1988 that joint army maneuvers on the "central front" were becoming irrelevant to the true security challenges that France and Germany would face. Forty years after they began to change from fierce enemies to close partners, France and Germany had yet to prove that they could transform their cooperation from symbolic reconciliation on one side of a Cold War alliance into a partnership actually capable of making common policy decisions and perhaps even executing joint military actions. To an extent greater than anyone could have predicted at the time, the end of the Cold War would give them the opportunity to do so.

Notes

[1] For a good discussion of the concept of strategic culture and its application to Germany, see Stephen F. Szabo, *The Changing Politics of German Security* (London: Pinter, 1990), pp. 1-22.

[2] The seminal study of Gaullist foreign policy is Stanley Hoffmann, *Decline or Renewal? France Since the 1930s* (New York: The Viking Press, 1974), especially chaps. 8 and 10. For a good general overview, see Edward Kolodziej, *French International Policy Under de Gaulle and Pompidou: The Politics of Grandeur* (Ithaca: Cornell University Press, 1974).

[3] France's concern with rank did not die with the end of the Cold War. As recently as March 1991, 72 percent of French people surveyed still believed that France was a great power. See "La France est-elle encore une grande puissance?" *L'Express*, March 1, 1991, pp. 28-33. On the pursuit of grandeur by de Gaulle and his successors, see Philip H. Gordon, *A Certain Idea of France: French Security Policy and the Gaullist Legacy* (Princeton, NJ: Princeton University Press, 1993).

[4] On West German foreign and security policy in the postwar period, see Wolfram F. Hanrieder, *Germany, America, Europe: Forty Years of German Foreign Policy* (New Haven: Yale University Press, 1989).

[5] Public opinion polls support the case that the French and Germans—right through the end of the Cold War—have had very different views of the use of military force. When asked in May 1991 whether they agreed with the statement that their country "must have a strong defense in order to defend its territory," 46 percent of French people surveyed "agreed strongly," in contrast to only 17 percent of the Germans. When asked whether war was sometimes necessary to protect a country's vital interests, 68 percent of the French "agreed strongly or somewhat," compared to 42 percent of the Germans. It is not surprising, then, that at the end of 1990, just before the Persian Gulf war began, 60 percent of the French supported

the use of military force to drive the Iraqi army out of Kuwait while only 22 percent of the Germans supported the use of force. For the first two polls, see the May 1991 Commissioned Personal Interview Surveys provided by the United States Information Agency. For the Gulf War poll results, see Dominique Dhombres, "Britanniques et Français restent les plus favorables au recours à la force," *Le Monde*, December 23-24, 1990, p. 3. For French and German public opinion toward security during the Cold War, see Gregory Flynn and Hans Rattinger, eds., *The Public and Atlantic Defense* (London, Croom Helm, 1985), chaps. 3-4.

[6] The literature on Franco-German security cooperation in the postwar period is extensive. For a few good overviews, see the two works cited in Note 1 as well as Karl Kaiser and Pierre Lellouche, eds., *Deutsch-französische Sicherheitspolitik* (Bonn: Forschungsinstitut der Deutschen Gesellschaft für Auswärtige Politik, 1986), published in French as *Le couple franco-allemand et la défense de l'Europe* (Paris: Institut Français des Relations Internationales, 1986); and David S. Yost, "Franco-German Defence Cooperation," in Stephen F. Szabo, ed., *The Bundeswehr and Western Security* (New York: St. Martin's Press, 1990), pp. 217-258.

[7] For de Gaulle's and other early French views of Franco-German reconciliation, see Pierre Maillard, *De Gaulle et l'Allemagne: Le rêve inachevé* (Paris: Plon, 1990), pp. 83-118; F. Roy Willis, *France, Germany and the New Europe: 1945-67*, rev. ed., (London: Oxford University Press, 1968), pp. 15-16; and Raymond Poidevin, "Der Faktor Europas in der Deutschlandpolitik Robert Schumans 1948/49," *Vierteljahreshefte für Zeitgeschichte* (July 1985). For de Gaulle's own claim that he sensed the need for Franco-German reconciliation as early as 1945, see the third volume of his war memoirs, Charles de Gaulle, *Salvation: 1944-46* (New York: Simon and Schuster, 1960), p. 235.

[8] See Jean-Pierre Rioux, *La France de la Quatrième République: L'ardeur et la nécessité, 1944-1952* (Paris: Editions du Seuil, 1980), pp. 202-204.

[9] Adenauer used the West's desperate need for German rearmament as leverage to get the occupation statutes lifted and restore Germany's place in the community of nations. On Adenauer's attitude toward the EDC, see Robert McGeehan, *The German Rearmament Question: American Diplomacy and European Defense After World War II* (Urbana IL: University of Illinois Press, 1971), pp. 141-143. Also see the discussions in Willis, *France, Germany and the New Europe*, pp. 136-137 and 153-155; and Hans-Peter Schwarz, *Adenauer: Der Aufstieg, 1876-1952* (Stuttgart: Deutsche Verlags-Anstalt, 1986), pp. 830-836.

[10] This is of course somewhat simplified and unfair, in that under the EDC France would have as much—or as little—control over its armed forces as Germany. However, the French perception was that they were giving up something they had (an independent national army), while the Germans were gaining something they did not have (an army *tout court*); thus the often-heard formula in France that the EDC "rearms Germany and disarms France." See Raymond Aron, "Historical Sketch of the Great Debate," in Raymond Aron and Daniel Lerner, eds., *France*

Defeats the EDC (New York: Frederick A. Praeger, 1957), pp. 2-21. For de Gaulle's views of the EDC, see Jean Touchard, *Le gaullisme: 1940-1969* (Paris: Editions du Seuil, 1978), pp. 115-117.

[11] After all these years, the best study of the EDC's downfall remains Aron and Lerner, eds., *France Defeats the EDC*. Also see Edward Fursdon, *The EDC: A History* (London: Macmillan, 1980); and for a German analysis based on newly available documents, Rolf Steininger, "Das Scheitern der EVG und der Beitritt der Bundesrepublik zur NATO," *Aus Politik und Zeitgeschichte*, supplement to *Das Parlament*, B 17/85 (1985), pp. 3-18.

[12] As part of its accession to the WEU, the Federal Republic agreed to restrictions on the numbers and types of conventional arms it could possess and to renounce the manufacture of atomic, biological, and chemical weapons (ABC weapons) on German soil. On the 1954 Paris accords providing for German accession to the WEU, see Alfred Grosser, *La IVe République et sa politique extérieure* (Paris: Armand Colin, 1961), pp. 320-326; and Hans Buchheim, *Deutschlandpolitik, 1949-72: Der politisch-diplomatische Prozess* (Stuttgart: Deutsche Verlags-Anstalt, 1984), p. 49. Adenauer's renunciation of ABC weapons was made in a declaration attached to Protocol No. 3 on the Control of Armaments, signed in Paris on October 23, 1954, amending the Brussels Treaty of 1948. For a text, see *NATO: Facts about the North Atlantic Treaty Organization* (Paris: NATO Information Service, 1965), p. 256.

[13] As Strauss liked to point out, nuclear cooperation with France did not technically violate Germany's 1954 pledges, which concerned only the production of atomic weapons *on German soil*, not participation in nuclear research somewhere else. See Wilfred L. Kohl, *French Nuclear Diplomacy* (Princeton NJ: Princeton University Press, 1971), pp. 54-61. On the nuclear cooperation issue in general, see Georges-Henri Soutou, "Les Accords de 1957 et 1958: vers une communauté stratégique et nucléaire entre la France, l'Allemagne et l'Italie?" *Matériaux pour l'histoire de notre temps*, no. 31 (April-June 1993): 1-12; Catherine McArdle Kelleher, *Germany and the Politics of Nuclear Weapons* (New York: Columbia University Press, 1975), pp. 104, 132, and 146-151; and the series of articles devoted to the subject in *Revue d'histoire diplomatique*, nos. 1-2 (1990).

[14] For a discussion of these episodes, see Jean Lacouture, *De Gaulle*, vol. 3, *Le Souverain, 1959-70* (Paris: Le Seuil, 1986), pp. 303-305.

[15] For the full text of the Elysée Treaty, as well as extensive information on its legacy, see the report of the coordinator of Franco-German cooperation, Rainer Barzel, *25 Jahre deutsch-französische Zusammenarbeit/25ans de coopération franco-allemande* (Bonn: Bundesrepublik Deutschland, Presse- und Informationsamt der Bundesregierung, November 1987). The defense clauses of the treaty can also be found in the annex of Kaiser and Lellouche, eds., *Deutsch-französische Sicherheitspolitik*, pp. 308-13 (or in the French version, *Le couple franco-allemand*, pp. 329-33). For an interesting commentary written for the treaty's 25th anniversary, see Hans-Peter Schwarz, *Eine Entente Elémentaire,*

rev. ed., Arbeitspapiere zur Internationalen Politik 47 (Bonn: Forschungsinstitut der Deutschen Gesellschaft für Auswärtige Politik, 1990).

[16] De Gaulle apparently cut off the nuclear discussions with Germany immediately upon his return to office and without study or discussion. See Kohl, *French Nuclear Diplomacy*, p. 63. On the tripartite affair and the diffidence from NATO, see Michael M. Harrison, *The Reluctant Ally: France and Atlantic Security* (Baltimore: The Johns Hopkins University Press, 1981), chaps. 1-4.

[17] For Adenauer's perspectives on the 1963 treaty, see Konrad Adenauer, *Erinnerungen: 1959-63* (Stuttgart: Deutsche Verlags-Anstalt, 1965), p. 205. For Adenauer's and other German reactions to de Gaulle's veto of Great Britain, see Willis, *France, Germany and the New Europe*, pp. 309-310. The unilateral veto seemed incompatible with the Elysée Treaty's call for France and Germany "to consult with each other before all important foreign policy questions." For de Gaulle's reaction to the Bundestag's preamble (which Jean Lacouture compared to an edition of Karl Marx's *Das Kapital* prefaced by Ronald Reagan), see Lacouture, *De Gaulle*, vol.3, *Le Souverain*, pp. 308-309.

[18] On de Gaulle's *Ostpolitik*, see Frédéric Bozo, "Paradigm Lost: The French Experience with Détente," in Richard Davy, ed., *European Détente: A Reappraisal* (London: Royal Institute of International Affairs, 1991); as well as Kolodziej, *French International Policy*, chap. 7.

[19] See Hanrieder, *Germany, America, Europe*, pp. 180-190.

[20] See, for example, Brandt adviser Egon Bahr's comment that the Eastern treaties were "the consequence of the treaties with the West," in Walter F. Hahn, "West Germany's Ostpolitik: The Grand Design of Egon Bahr," *Orbis* (winter 1973):878.

[21] Georges Pompidou's words, cited in Daniel Colard, "Convergences et divergences politiques," *Documents* 2 (1974):95.

[22] See Jean Klein, "Mythes et réalités de la défense de l'Europe," *Politique étrangère* 2 (1983):320-321.

[23] A possible exception would be the (ultimately successful) negotiation of the Valentin-Ferber Accords that provided for practical military cooperation between French and German troops in NATO if the French government agreed that French troops could be used. But when put in perspective, the fact that such agreements were necessary in the first place only underlined the limits to Franco-German military cooperation and integration at the time. See Yost, "Franco-German Defence Cooperation," p. 220.

[24] In fact, Méry never really promised a nuclear guarantee for Germany, but he did send a message that France's defense interests began at the Elbe rather than the Rhine, and that France would be prepared to use its conventional forces (and perhaps even tactical nuclear weapons) to defend those interests. See Général d'Armée G. Méry, "Une armée pour quoi faire et comment?" *Défense nationale* 32 (June 1976):11-24. English excerpts from Méry can be found as "Comments by General Guy Méry, March 15, 1976," *Survival* 18, no. 5 (September-October 1976):226-228. For the language of the military program law, see Assemblée

Nationale, "Loi No. 76-531 du 19 juin 1976 portant approbation de la programmation militaire pour les années 1977-1982," *Journal officiel de la République française* (June 20, 1976):3,700.

[25] See, for example, Chief of Staff Méry's comment, "It would be extremely dangerous for [France] deliberately to hold herself aloof from [the] first battle, in the course of which [her] own security would in fact be at stake." See Méry, "Comments," p. 227. On Giscard's military policies in general, see Gordon, *Certain Idea of France*, chap. 4.

[26] According to Schmidt, Giscard had told him in July 1980, "I want to take great steps together with you after my reelection; until then let us please not disturb French public opinion." The chancellor answered that he would "be as ready to do that next year as this. But please do not forget that my term in office has its limits." Schmidt's sense of what domestic politics had in store seems to have been more prescient than Giscard's. See Helmut Schmidt, *Die Deutschen und ihre Nachbarn* (Berlin: Goldman, 1990), p. 320.

[27] See the "Déclaration du Président de la République à l'issue des consultations franco-allemandes des 21 et 22 octobre 1982 à Bonn," in Ministère des Relations Extérieures, *La politique étrangère de la France: Textes et documents. Octobre-novembre-décembre 1982* (Paris: Documentation Française, 1983).

[28] For details on the Franco-German Security Commission, see André Adrets (pseudonym of a former defense ministry official), "Les relations franco-allemandes et le fait nucléaire dans une Europe divisée," *Politique étrangère* 3 (fall 1984): 649-664.

[29] See Jacques Isnard, "Relance spectaculaire de la coopération militarie franco-allemande," *Le Monde*, May 30, 1984, p. 1.

[30] See the January 20, 1983, Bundestag speech printed as "Il faut que la guerre demeure impossible," in François Mitterrand, *Réflexions sur la politique extérieure de la France* (Paris: Fayard, 1986), pp. 183-208.

[31] On the agreement to "relaunch" the WEU, see *Le Monde*, February 25, 1984.

[32] See Charles Hernu, "Face à la logique des blocs, une France indépendante et solidaire," *Défense nationale* (December 1982):17.

[33] See Hernu cited in *Le Monde*, November 5, 1983, p. 9.

[34] See "L'offensive Giraud," *L'Express*, July 10-16, 1987, p. 40. Also see President Mitterrand's warning that American disengagement was "a real danger" (interview with Mitterrand by Jean Daniel entitled "La Stratégie, par François Mitterrand," *Le Nouvel observateur*, December 18-24, 1987, p. 25; subsequently cited as Mitterrand, "La Stratégie").

[35] See, for example, Christoph Bertram, "Europe's Security Dilemmas," *Foreign Affairs* 65, no. 5 (summer 1987):942-957; Alfred Dregger, "Entwurf einer Sicherheitspolitik zur Selbstbehauptung Europas," *Europäische Wehrkünde* 12 (December 1987); Helmut Schmidt, "Deutsch-französische Zusammenarbeit in der Sicherheitspolitik," *Europa-Archiv* 11 (1987):303-312. For a general discussion of German views, see Hanrieder, *Germany, America, Europe*, pp. 113-130.

[36] The statement issued by Mitterrand following the meetings announced: "Within the limits imposed by the extreme rapidity of such decision, the President of the Republic declares himself disposed to consult the Chancellor of the FRG on the possible employment of prestrategic French weapons on German territory. He notes that the decision cannot be shared in this matter. The President of the Republic indicates that he has decided, with the Chancellor of the FRG, to equip himself with technical means for immediate and reliable consultation in time of crisis." See the February 28, 1986, declaration published in *Le Monde*, March 2-3, 1986, p. 4. Excerpts from the declaration were published in English as "Press conference of François Mitterrand, President of the Republic of France," March 7, 1986, *Survival* 4 (1986):367.

[37] *Mehr Schein als Sein* might best be translated as "more appearance than reality."

[38] See Genscher's January 2, 1987, speech to the World Economic Forum in Davos, Switzerland, published as "Nehmen wir Gorbatshow ernst, nehmen wir ihn beim Wort," in Hans-Dietrich Genscher, *Wir wollen ein Europäisches Deutschland* (Berlin: Goldman, 1991), pp. 135-148.

[39] For the polling data as well as a good discussion of changing German attitudes toward the Soviet Union, see Szabo, *Changing Politics*, pp. 47-51.

[40] For Chirac's position, see "M. Chirac prône la vigilance à l'égard de l'Union soviétique," *Le Monde*, March 2, 1988, p. 2. For Mitterrand, see Claire Tréan, "M. Mitterrand se déclare hostile à la modernisation des armes nucléaires de l'OTAN," *Le Monde*, February 27, 1988.

[41] See Mitterrand's remarks in "La stratégie nucléaire de la France s'adresse à l'agresseur et à lui seul," *Le Monde*, October 21, 1987; and "Le chef de l'Etat confirme son intention de réviser la doctrine sur l'emploi des armes préstratégiques françaises," *Le Monde*, October 22, 1987.

[42] See Gordon, *Certain Idea of France*, chap. 6.

[43] See Peter Schmidt, "The Franco-German Defense and Security Council," *Aussenpolitik* (English edition) 40, no. 4 (1989): 367-368.

[44] See Christian Millotat and Jean-Claude Philippot, "Le jumelage franco-allemand pour la sécurité de l'Europe," *Défense nationale* (October 1990):67.

2

The Franco-German Partnership and the Western Alliance, 1989-1994

Post-Cold War Challenges to the Franco-German Partnership

From the perspective of the 1990s, the numerous examples of Franco-German military cooperation from 1950 to 1989 that seemed so important at the time suddenly seem anachronistic. The discussions of an extended French nuclear deterrent (that the Germans never really asked for and the French were unable to give); the various Franco-German military maneuvers (that demonstrated France's commitment to the alliance but paled in comparison with the scale of maneuvers within NATO as a whole); the creation of defense commissions and councils (that provided useful forums for discussion but had little impact on actual policy); and the increasing French declarations of commitment to Germany's defense (that should have gone without saying) were all mostly rhetorical or symbolic. Symbols, of course, are important in security policy and have played a great role in the case of France and Germany. But during a period when Western defense was provided overwhelmingly by a German-American army on the central front backed up by U.S. nuclear weapons, Franco-German security cooperation must be seen as far more important to the political reconciliation of the two countries than it was in terms of providing actual defense.

31

Franco-German cooperation in the post-Cold War era seems likely to be both more difficult and more important than in the past. For four main reasons, structural changes in the international system challenge not only the partnership's ability to hold together but also its capacity to address and confront the true security concerns of the emerging era.

The first factor making Franco-German cooperation more challenging than in the past is the disappearance of the ideological and military threat from the Soviet Union. The Soviet threat, of course, was by no means the only factor that brought and held France and Germany together during the Cold War. To argue that it was would be to misunderstand the many other factors leading to Franco-German reconciliation after 1945—the French and Germans teamed up not only to stand against the Soviets but also to conclude their repeated fratricide, to enhance their economic situation, to stand up to the two superpowers, and to contain German power.[1] As the last chapter showed, however, it would be equally wrong to deny that the Soviet occupation of Eastern Europe and military threat to Western Europe made an important contribution to the French and German strategic partnership during the Cold War. The Soviet threat was the main reason France was willing to accept German rearmament in the first place; it was the focus of *all* Franco-German security initiatives during the 1960s, 1970s and 1980s; and for the first time in history it provided France and Germany with an external adversary that was not each other. With the security threats to Western Europe now more heterogeneous and subjective than during the era of the clear threat from the East, French and German security cooperation is not as natural as it was during the Cold War.

Second, the challenge to Franco-German security cooperation will henceforth be greater because Europe's guarantor during the Cold War years, the United States, is unlikely to be willing or able to play the "protectorate" role that prevailed in what might be called the *Pax Americana*. Having spent nearly $3 trillion on defense during the 1980s alone—and having added to the national debt by a similar amount during that time—the United States entered the post-Cold War era with a number of serious social and economic problems at home and a sense that these problems had become a greater threat to American interests than any foreign military power. The November 1992 presidential election of Bill Clinton, the young governor of a small southern state, who had emphasized economic and social policy in the campaign and who had little experience in international leadership, over the incumbent George Bush, a man of vast experience, talent, and interest in foreign affairs, seemed symbolic of a shift in American priorities from a preoccupation with global security and international leadership to a preoccupation with domestic affairs. The United States continues to have important security interests in Europe and around the world, and there is no reason to believe that it will soon withdraw from international affairs (or that it could even if it wanted to). But the global and European security role of the United States will undoubtedly be less prominent than when it was engaged in a global ideological battle with the Soviet Union and when America's own economic and military power was unchallenged throughout the Western world. This logically implies a greater contribution to European and Atlantic security from the European allies of the United States and most of all from Germany and France, Western Europe's two largest and richest states.

Third, the Franco-German security partnership has become more difficult than in the past because German unification threw off a fundamental balance that contributed to the rapprochement of Germany and France. As Stanley Hoffmann has described it, the Franco-German partnership had always been based on a sort of *équilibre des deséquilibres*—France and Germany were well-matched because French military and nuclear power compensated for Germany's economic strength.[2] During the Cold War, a divided Germany still trying to cope with its Nazi past desperately needed a close partnership with France as a contribution to its democratic legitimacy and to its security in the East. With unification, however, some of Germany's past need for France has been diminished: Germany is now united, fully-sovereign, bigger, no longer under a direct military threat, and led by a generation of leaders born too late to bear any possible responsibility for World War II. The emergence of a Germany now 41 percent more populous than France, and with an economy 39 percent greater than France's, undermines the fundamental balance that once existed between Western Europe's two largest states.

Finally, the challenge to Franco-German security cooperation is greater than in previous years because the task at hand has become more difficult: No longer is the question the relatively simple one (though it obviously did not seem simple at the time) of defending against (an unlikely) Warsaw Pact aggression or providing for nuclear deterrence, but it is the task of responding to a whole new array of threats to French and German interests that have emerged from the end of the Cold War. The emergence of numerous ethnic disputes in Southern and Eastern Europe that were set loose by the end of Soviet domination (some of which have already broken out into civil wars); the population explosion in Africa and especially North Africa that could lead to social instability and the rise of Islamic fundamentalism; the proliferation of weapons of mass destruction, long-range delivery systems, and high-tech conventional weapons; uncertainty with the stability of the reform process in Russia; and the potential for mass immigration stemming from economic failure to Europe's south and east all lead to the sustainable proposition that the end of the Cold War has not enhanced the security of France and Germany but made it more precarious.[3]

None of the challenges discussed here guarantees that the Franco-German partnership will weaken, and "neo-realist" predictions of West European disintegration in the post-Cold War world underestimate the partnership's resilience.[4] The structure of the international system is important in determining national policy, but looking at structure alone overlooks other factors such as personal commitments, historic memories, multinational institutions and—most importantly—a realization of inescapable interdependence. These factors make the scenarios that predict the disintegration of the Franco-German partnership or the return to bilateral conflict seem improbable.

Still, analysts who suspected that the early 1990s would not be the peaceful, harmonious era of Western cooperation and unification envisaged in the euphoric atmosphere of 1989 and 1990 have been proven more perspicacious than some of their detractors. Although we may not yet "miss the Cold War," as one of these analysts predicted we soon would, we do have to admit that Western security cooperation has so far been more difficult than in the past.[5] The first four post-Cold War years have revealed diverse roles and interests among the Western allies in the Gulf War coalition; serious debates between France and Germany and within the West about the future of longstanding security organizations; different conceptions in Paris and Bonn over how to ensure security and stability in Eastern Europe and the former Soviet Union; and, perhaps most importantly, a ghastly civil war in the heart of Europe that has divided the allies and led to mutual recrimination and resentment. Compared to these recent challenges, Cold War tasks such as finding common positions on arms control, agreeing on burden sharing or creating a Franco-German brigade seem relatively unproblematic. As the following case studies will demonstrate, the disappearance of the Soviet threat, the unification of Germany, the relative disengagement from Europe of the United States, and the emergence of instability to Europe's east and south have seriously begun to challenge the ability of the Franco-German couple—and the West as a whole—to function effectively.

How well, then, has the Franco-German security partnership functioned in the post-Cold War world so far? Is there evidence that France and Germany can meet contemporary security crises with common policies and common means? And what has been the effect of recent Franco-German cooperation on the rest of the alliance? The following case studies examine French and German security cooperation with each other and with their major allies since 1989.

The National Lessons of the Persian Gulf War

The first post-Cold War test of the Franco-German security partnership was the kind of test it was least prepared for. Thirty years of Franco-German security cooperation never included preparation for "out-of-area" crises, and when Iraq invaded Kuwait on August 2, 1990, the Franco-German partnership was relegated to no more than a marginal role. Rather than demonstrating the fruits of cooperation or convergence, the war only underlined the enduring differences between the two countries as well as their different military and political relations with their allies.

The Franco-German couple had no real role to play in the Gulf because of the two very different historical, cultural, and military traditions of the two countries. French policy in the Gulf was greatly influenced, for example, by a supposed "special relationship" with the Arab world and in particular with Iraq. France was Iraq's largest arms supplier throughout the 1980s, and from 1978 to 1988 it had depended on Iraq for no less than one-third of it foreign arms sales. For many in the ruling Socialist party, moreover, Iraq had long been seen as a secular bastion against the religious fundamentalism supported by Iran. Numerous French political and industrial leaders since the 1970s (including twice-prime minister Jacques Chirac) had maintained good relations with Saddam Hussein, and the French defense minister at the time of the Gulf War, Jean-Pierre Chevènement, was no less than the founding president of the France-Iraq Friendship Society. With 2 to 3 million Arabs (whose loyalties in the conflict were difficult to predict) living in France and with special concern for relations with North Africa (where the populations were clearly pro-Iraq), French leaders had to be even more careful than others to demonstrate that they would do everything possible to avoid war. All of this helps to explain President Mitterrand's diplomatic maneuvering at the UN and with Iraq.

Another important factor determining French policy in the Gulf was France's desire to demonstrate its *rang*, or standing in the world.[6] A permanent member of the UN Security Council, France considered itself a significant global and military power and had a long history of involvement and interests in the Middle East. After thirty years of ostentatiously proclaiming its military and diplomatic independence, moreover, France had no intention of abandoning all political prerogative to Washington and allowing the United States to dictate international policy in a global crisis. At the same time, if war did come, *rang* meant that France could not be seen as having been left on the sidelines while other states (such as Great Britain) played important military roles. Military participation in the Gulf War would also be a way to reaffirm France's role as at least a middle-sized world power, all the more important in wake of the East European revolutions of 1989 and 1990 and the German unification process during which France had felt marginalized. Once war became inevitable, the notion of *rang* pushed France in the direction of participation rather than abstention, and Mitterrand did not fail to assert in his first major speech after the Gulf War that "France had upheld her role and her rank." Notably, Mitterrand emphasized France's national role in his speech, and failed to mention Europe at all.[7]

In contrast to France, Germany had neither the means nor the inclination to play a high-profile diplomatic or active military role in the Gulf. Since World War II, the Federal Republic had avoided global military responsibilities and limited its diplomatic and security policy primarily to Western and Central Europe. The Federal Republic had no history of involvement in Persian Gulf security, and, with neither a permanent seat on the UN Security Council nor a tradition of military intervention abroad, it had no particular feeling of responsibility for security crises beyond Europe. Since the early 1980s, moreover, German governments had interpreted their constitution as prohibiting the deployment of military forces beyond the "zone" covered by the North Atlantic Treaty, an interpretation reaffirmed by the Kohl government three weeks after the Iraqi invasion of Kuwait.[8]

It should also be remembered that the Gulf crisis broke out just as the German unification process was coming to a head: Inter-German currency union took place in July 1990, Iraq invaded Kuwait in August, unification was in October, and the air war began in January 1991. This coincidence of history not only diverted attention in Germany from the Gulf crisis and limited the financial contribution Germans felt they could make to the war effort (a limit eventually overcome by international pressure), but it also made Germans all the more cautious about getting too deeply involved in the war. Whereas the new Germany was now under growing pressure from its allies to take on new responsibilities in the world, it also felt obliged (because of those same allies) to show restraint in its first foreign policy actions as a unified state. With the Soviets yet to ratify the two-plus-four treaty and the French, British, and even Americans vigilantly watching the united Germany's potential power, leaders in Bonn had to be careful before quickly embarking on global military activities. Reactions to Germany's later attempt to play an active role in the conflict in former Yugoslavia tend to confirm the wisdom of this reserved approach.

In light of such dissimilar historical, political, and cultural backgrounds, it should not have been surprising that French and German policies in the Gulf differed as well. French policy in the Gulf War can best be described as a sort of "two-track" approach; on one hand an attempt to pursue an independent mediation role between Iraq and the Western allies, and, on the other hand, full participation in the allied military coalition against Iraq. As part of the first track (meditation), France initially sought to avoid a military role in the conflict, conducted secret exploratory negotiations with Saddam Hussein's brother-in-law, sent presidential emissaries to Baghdad and, most significantly, initiated a number of independent peace proposals, including a last-minute (January 14, 1991) attempt to allow Iraq a possible way out of the coming war.[9] The simultaneous second track (firmness) included repeated and resolute declarations of solidarity with the allies, a full implementation of sanctions against Iraq, an early deployment of military forces to the Gulf to enforce those sanctions, and, eventually, the deployment of a 12,000-man land-based division. French forces participated in both the air and ground aspects of the allied campaign and executed their given missions extremely effectively.

The German role in the Gulf War coalition differed greatly from France's both in the diplomatic and military domains.[10] Diplomatically, in contrast to France's independent mediation efforts and UN Security Council role, Germany was content to follow along with the coalition's sanctions and to limit its role to financial contributions. Under pressure from the allies, those contributions eventually reached an estimated DM 18 billion, nearly 10 percent of the total international expenditure for the war and its consequences.[11] The German military role in the Gulf was actually far more extensive than was first made known. Germany provided critical support in aiding with the deployment of American and British forces from bases in the Federal Republic to the Gulf, shipped surplus military supplies to the allies stationed in Saudi Arabia, supplied tank and artillery ammunition for American and British forces, sent (after much internal debate) an AlphaJet squadron and units equipped with Hawk and Roland surface-to-air missiles to Turkey as part of NATO's Allied Command Europe (ACE) Mobile Force, and, after the war was over, deployed minesweepers to the Persian

Gulf. Despite all this unpublicized effort, however, it remains true that Germany took no direct military action in the Gulf and, in this sense, played a role more similar to that of Western allies like Belgium or Holland than to that of Great Britain, the United States, or indeed, France. Looking objectively at the national and institutional roles in the Gulf, it must be concluded that the Franco-German partnership played hardly any role at all.

For many of the Western allies, the absence of a Franco-German role in the Gulf War was not a disappointment but in fact was rather welcome. The war reassured the more "Atlanticist" allies that Franco-German bilateralism would not prevent the functioning of the Atlantic alliance and that NATO—even if unofficially—remained the West's primary security organization. Great Britain, concerned that an April 1990 Franco-German proposal to create a European political union would weaken the Atlantic alliance, was particularly relieved to see NATO's utility confirmed and the importance of the American connection underscored. Similarly worried by President Bush's May 1989 call for Germany to become America's new "partner in leadership," the British were pleased to have an opportunity to show the functioning of the original "special relationship" and to demonstrate that they, not the Germans, were America's most dependable Atlantic partner when it counted most. Prime Minister John Major pointedly made the distinction between the British and other European roles in the House of Commons on January 22, 1991:

> There is undoubtedly considerable disparity in the extent to which individual European countries have committed themselves to the problems of the Gulf. Political union and a common foreign and security policy in Europe would have to go beyond statement and extend to action. Clearly, Europe is not ready for that.[12]

For the United States itself, the Gulf War was a demonstration that it was indeed the world's only remaining superpower and that Europe remained critically dependent on American military might. As U.S. NATO ambassador William Taft put it, "The effective, coordinated military operations in the Gulf were made possible by the fact that NATO had for years executed peacetime common training, armaments programs and joint maneuvers and that it had developed common norms and procedures."[13] There was some satisfaction in Washington, moreover, that military force seemed to have been revalued as a potential tool of international affairs, and even a bit of *Schadenfreude* at seeing the weakness of the European

Community's (EC) supposed "common foreign and security policy." Many Americans believed the Gulf War showed the dependence of exclusively European military cooperation on the Atlantic alliance and hoped the French and Germans would reach the same conclusions.[14]

In fact, France and Germany did not dispute the British and American inferences about the continued importance of military strength, Europe's military impotence, the need for the United States, and Britain's special relation with Washington. They did, however, reach a very different conclusion from these discoveries: Rather than admitting that a European security identity was an unachievable goal, many French and Germans decided it would have to be more seriously built. The Gulf War prompted a number of French and German calls for increased Franco-German security cooperation, including a February 1991 proposal by Roland Dumas and Hans-Dietrich Genscher and a joint initiative sponsored that same month by the Christian Democratic Union's (CDU) foreign policy spokesman Karl Lamers and Socialist member of the European Parliament Gérard Fuchs.[15] The same conclusion was reached by the French president of the EC Commission, Jacques Delors, who argued in March 1991 that the "limitations of the European Community in the Gulf [were] yet another argument for moving towards a form of political union embracing a common foreign and security policy."[16]

The differences between the French and German policies and attitudes in the Gulf War should not be exaggerated. At the very least it is important to recognize that, after their initial hesitations, both France and Germany gave unmitigated support to the UN coalition, provided military support in one form or another, and carefully avoided any temptation of unilateralism. French and German public opinion before and during the war was less different than their national policies, and the very experience of the war probably tended to push French and German thinking closer together on security policy issues than to pull them apart. Many observers in both countries concluded that if Europe was to have any influence in international politics, it would have to coordinate its foreign and security policies and means better than in the past.

Still, for two intimate neighbors who claimed to represent a security "couple" and who hoped to form the nucleus of a European defense, the Gulf War must have been a sobering experience. It demonstrated that French and German strategic cultures were still very different despite thirty years of cooperation, that their ability to lead a coherent European security policy was severely limited, and that large-scale military operations were beyond the range of actions of which France and Germany were then capable.

Neither the existence of Franco-German defense and security councils and commissions nor the regular meetings of high government officials nor the ongoing discussions of a common European foreign and security policy were enough to prevent French and German policies in the Gulf crisis from being based almost exclusively on questions of domestic politics, perceptions, and interests. Perhaps it is unfair to judge the Franco-German security relationship on an event as unique and as far from Europe as the Gulf War, but no one can be sure that this has been the last such war or that, if there is another, the United States will be as ready, willing, or able to lead the international response as in the past.

Institutions: The Debate About the Eurocorps

One of the most difficult challenges facing the West after the disappearance of the Soviet threat was the transformation of European and transatlantic security organizations. Having seen a large scale military conflict break out in the Persian Gulf and watching another emerge in the Balkans, the Western allies sensed that security institutions and plans would still be necessary in the post-cold War world, but they differed over what they should look like. The primary point of contention—which led to sometimes acrimonious transatlantic and intra-European disputes—was the extent to which Europe and the Europeans should have their own security "identity" and institutions within the overall Western alliance. And just as in the early 1960s, debates between proponents of an "Atlantic Europe" (Harold Macmillan, John F. Kennedy, Paul-Henri Spaak, and Joseph Luns) and supporters of a "European Europe" (Charles de Gaulle and Konrad Adenauer), the early-1990s debate saw the United States, Great Britain, and the Netherlands on one side, with France and Germany (ostensibly, at least) on the other.

Beginning with the April 1990 "political union" initiative, France and Germany put forth a series of broad proposals for creating a true "European security identity" within the framework of the European Community.[17] According to the Franco-German plans, this identity would initially be formed around the Western European Union (WEU)—10 of the 12 EC members—but would eventually "fuse" with the EC itself into a complete "political union," perhaps by 1998 when the WEU's original 50-year statute runs out. Whereas some of France and Germany's European partners (in particular Great Britain and the Netherlands) had argued that the WEU should simply be a "bridge" between the EC and NATO, France and Germany emphasized its direct, "organic" links with the EC.[18] At the Community's Maastricht summit on political and economic union in December 1991, a compromise was reached: Summit leaders accepted that the EC would for the first time deal with military-security issues and that the WEU would be directly linked to the EC, but also declared only that the EC "might in time" create its own common defense and that the WEU would do more to "act in conformity" with NATO. The historic "Atlantic" vs. "European" differences were papered over at Maastricht, but by no means resolved.[19]

The most significant of the Franco-German initiatives on the European defense identity was the Kohl-Mitterrand proposal of October 14, 1991, to develop the existing Franco-German brigade into a complete European army corps. The original proposal was, in fact, no more than a two-line footnote at the end of a long letter on political union, but it soon took on much larger proportions.[20] Much like the April 1990 "political union" proposal, this initiative—reportedly advanced without the consultation of the respective French and German defense and foreign ministries—seemed to be an attempt by Mitterrand and Kohl to use their special relationship to give substance and political momentum and to a process that would be more difficult to organize and debate among the twelve EC states. Not unlike the 1963 Elysée Treaty itself, which came on the heels of a failed "political union" program for the then six EC members (the Fouchet Plan), the Eurocorps plan reflected French and German willingness to move ahead of their partners with the hope of subsequently drawing those partners in their wake.[21]

The reactions among the allies to the Eurocorps initiative were mixed and largely predictable. Some European countries, such as Belgium, Spain, and Luxembourg, showed sympathy for the idea and their support for European integration outweighed their reservations; Belgium even decided in March 1993 to join the Eurocorps and to contribute an armored division.[22] But others were considerably more skeptical. The United Kingdom put forth traditional reservations about the potential for weakening NATO, and some of the smaller European partners—notably the Netherlands and Italy— did not like the way the supposedly "European" corps was presented—as a bilateral announcement without any forewarning or consultation. Reflecting longstanding concerns about a Franco-German "axis" in Europe, Dutch foreign minister Hans van den Broek complained about being "subject to Franco-German consensus," and Italian defense minister Virginio Rognoni argued that "bilateral agreements are not the way to build a common European defense."[23] Whereas the corps was largely well received across the French political spectrum, a number of German commentators, particularly in the opposition SPD, criticized both the presentation and the content of the corps. Some SPD spokesmen saw in it a French plan to drag Germany along on its international military adventures and argued that German forces should be integrated only in NATO or the UN.[24]

The United States, too, was at best ambivalent toward the Eurocorps proposal.[25] Some American officials, especially in the Pentagon (often more relaxed toward European initiatives than the State Department) were generally supportive of the Franco-German initiative. Secretary of Defense Dick Cheney called the proposal "basically sound," Chairman of the Joint Chiefs of Staff Colin Powell suggested European units like the corps would be "politically and militarily well equipped to deal with interregional crises, humanitarian means and peacekeeping," and NATO SACEUR John Galvin, while expressing some misgivings about command structures, urged Congress to support the Eurocorps because "we want the Europeans to grow stronger without loosening their Atlantic ties."[26] Many Americans, however—especially in the administration—saw it as needless at best and at worst as potentially damaging to the NATO alliance. U.S. ambassador to Bonn Robert Kimmit reportedly protested before the chancellery, National Security adviser Brent Scowcroft wrote a sharp letter to chancellor Kohl complaining that Germany could undermine the Atlantic alliance, and U.S. ambassador to NATO William Taft IV suggested in a speech in Brussels, on the very day of the Franco-German summit in La Rochelle, that the Franco-German corps would be "inconsistent" with NATO structures because of France's independent role.[27] Taft claimed that the United States supported a European pillar, "but one that does not duplicate the Alliance, one that operates within the Alliance to do Alliance tasks and outside the Alliance only where it wishes to take on new missions."[28] That these views reflected the thinking of President Bush himself was made clear by his impromptu remarks at the NATO summit in Rome, just one month after the Franco-German corps was proposed: "If, my friends," declared Bush with the French and Germans clearly in mind, "your ultimate aim is to provide independently for your own defense, the time to tell us is today."[29] American negotiations with France over the relationship of the corps with NATO became so tense at one point that Secretary of State James Baker reportedly asked his French counterpart Roland Dumas, "Are you for us or against us?"[30]

Since the initially vague Franco-German proposal, details about the corps' structure, size, participants, and missions have gradually been worked out.[31]

The corps, expected to become operational in 1995, will consist of up to 45,000 troops—the first French armored division stationed at Baden-Baden (approximately 12,000 troops), two German mechanized brigades (12,000), an armored mechanized Belgian division (12,000), the Franco-German joint brigade (4,200), and logistical and communications units. It will operate under a rotating command structure among the three participating countries and will have a permanent headquarters of several hundred officers in Strasbourg, France. While the corps will have an integrated command structure even in peacetime, the deployment of any of its forces will still depend on national decisions to do so, and division-size units will remain strictly national, except for the truly integrated Franco-German joint brigade.[32] The corps' missions, first announced officially at the May 1992 Franco-German summit in La Rochelle, France, will be: (1)the defense of Western Europe in the context of article 5 of the NATO and WEU treaties; (2)peacekeeping and peacemaking; and (3)humanitarian tasks.[33]

One of the most difficult and controversial aspects of the corps has been its relationship with NATO and its integrated commands, a question that produced differences not only between the corps' Franco-German sponsors and their allies, but between the French and Germans themselves. Whereas Germany (all of whose troops are integrated into NATO anyway) wanted a close NATO link, France (whose forces are not in the integrated commands) had reservations. French officials never opposed the idea of the corps acting as part of NATO under certain contingencies, but they insisted on three conditions: that if the corps were placed under NATO command it should go "as a unit" and not be broken into constituent parts; that the relationship between the corps and NATO not be based on permanent peacetime integration but rather "operational control" (which allows for military units to be placed under foreign command for a specific and predetermined mission and time); and that the forces in the corps, while "double hatted," be loyal first to the Eurocorps and only secondarily to NATO if the corps' political leaders should so decide. In response to the French conditions, NATO leaders such as SACEUR John Galvin argued that independent European structures would create force redundancies, cause confusion in command structures, and complicate military planning.[34] Germany was caught in a familiar position of trying to placate both Washington and Paris and often found itself making somewhat contradictory promises to both sides on the "priority" of the corps' forces.[35]

After long and sometimes very difficult negotiations during 1992, most of these questions were resolved by an agreement among NATO SACEUR John Shalikashvili, German general inspector Klaus Naumann, and French chief of staff Jacques Lanxade at the end of November 1992. The accord was approved by the NATO council on December 22 and signed by the three parties on January 21, 1993.[36] Under the agreement, the Eurocorps can be used under the "operational command" of NATO, a procedure that gives the SACEUR authority to decide where and when to use it after getting authorization from France and Germany. As an expression of a European defense identity, however, the corps is "normally" only to be used as a unit (*en tant que tel*) and under the command of the corps' general; it can only be split up with the agreement of the Franco-German Security and Defense Council.[37] Most significant from the point of view of the alliance was that France agreed that the corps could come under NATO command not only for European defense but for peacekeeping missions as well, a task France had once opposed bringing into NATO's scope. This relatively positive result of long negotiations seems to indicate an underlying desire among all of the allies to cooperate, even when their perspectives and priorities diverge.

Nonetheless, the disagreement between the French and Germans over the Eurocorps' relationship with NATO reflected enduring philosophical differences between the two countries over the organization of Western security and the Atlantic alliance. From the French point of view, the Eurocorps would represent the first step toward truly independent European capacities for scenarios in which the United States would be unable or unwilling to act, and function as a means to influence more heavily the decisions of the United States when it did act. Numerous French leaders have claimed to be uncertain whether the Americans would remain in Europe and whether they would be as prepared in the future to lead European security as they had been during the Cold War.[38] The corps would thus be a basis for a future European army with autonomous capabilities for defense within Europe, peacekeeping and peacemaking tasks, and force projection abroad.

The German conception of the corps, in contrast, emphasized its role in organizing a better European contribution to the Atlantic alliance and, importantly, in drawing France closer to NATO. German officials repeatedly stated that they could not imagine the Eurocorps ever acting without the United States and often described it as a "second best" solution to full Euro-Atlantic integration. As one German diplomat put it: "We would have preferred that France simply reintegrate with NATO and that NATO serve as the West's primary security organization. But the French aren't willing to do that, so we took the next best thing."[39] This comment would seem to belie the often heard French assertion that (as one senior official in

Paris put it) "the Germans share every one of our concerns toward the Americans, only we have the courage to [express them]."[40] Indicatively, when the Eurocorps issue was finally settled with the Lanxade-Naumann-Shalikashvili accord, French officials congratulated themselves at having sold Germany on its conception of European defense while the Germans displayed satisfaction at having brought France closer to NATO.[41]

Of all the Franco-German security initiatives of the past thirty years, the proposal to integrate tens of thousands of their forces under a common command is clearly the most concrete. It not only demonstrates a symbolic political commitment to a common security strategy, but more important, actually provides the first real attempt to build the means to implement that strategy. The Eurocorps represents the first French acceptance of the concept of multinational military integration since 1958, allows for the first permanent stationing ever of German military forces on French soil (through the officers at the headquarters in Strasbourg), and provides a means for the continued presence of French troops in Germany, whose withdrawal had previously been announced on the grounds that they no longer had a legitimate legal or political justification.[42] On the German side, the acceptance of a military unit with international peacekeeping and peacemaking as a declared mission represents a new commitment to play an international security role and, importantly, to do so in a multilateral European context.[43] In all these ways, the Eurocorps must be seen as a step forward on the long road toward Franco-German unification in the security domain.

At the same time, one is obliged to conclude that the short- to medium-term impact of the corps will be very limited. Indeed, when one considers the three announced missions of the Eurocorps, it is difficult to imagine when or how it might usefully be employed. It seems implausible that the corps would really play an independent role in direct West European defense under article 5 (an implausible scenario itself), and it seems unlikely that France and Germany would choose to undertake peacekeeping, peacemaking, or even humanitarian missions that their allies had rejected. So far, in fact, France has been more likely to undertake such actions along with the United Kingdom (as in Yugoslavia) or the United States (as in the Persian Gulf or Somalia) than with the Federal Republic. The Eurocorps, moreover, is a good demonstration of why many of France's and Germany's allies find the Franco-German couple so problematic: It was announced with no input from the allies and, whatever the virtues and possibilities of "double hatting," it does tend to create force redundancies and complicate the command structures of the European security institutions already in place.

As a contribution to the European security identity, it risks creating—as many American officials fear and as many French officials explicitly seek— a European "caucus" within NATO that would make it difficult for the United States to influence European decisions once they are taken. As David Yost has explained, "If the United States is going to be involved in crash landings, it will want to be in on take-offs as well."[44]

In short, while the allies should welcome France's step toward integration in the alliance and Germany's toward participation in the range of military contingencies, it is difficult to see the Eurocorps as a major addition to the security instruments at Europe's disposal. Like many previous Franco-German security initiatives, this latest one is a good symbol of commitment and cooperation and a reasonable first step toward a worthy goal. If it is ever to develop into a truly useful means of implementing common security policies, however, France and Germany will have to find a way to agree on the policy before being able to use the means. The next two case studies raise questions about their ability to do that.

Ensuring Security and Stability in Eastern Europe

One of the areas in which French and German security policy cooperation has proven most difficult—and at the same time the area where their cooperation is perhaps most important—is Eastern Europe.[45] During the Cold War, aside from occasional national experiments with détente during the 1960s and 1970s, French and German policies toward the East were fundamentally similar, and the scope for divergence was highly circumscribed: Both countries sought to protect themselves against a possible Warsaw Pact invasion or a case of political blackmail, and, after the early 1970s, both obliquely supported—even while protesting against—the political status quo. Germans could make special efforts for their "compatriots" in the German Democratic Republic (GDR), and France could claim a right to nuclear power discussions with the USSR or historic special relationships in Eastern Europe, but it was the Russians who kept the peace in Eastern Europe during the Cold War, not the French and the Germans.

The end of the Cold War and German unification have increased German interests, responsibilities, and freedom of maneuver in Eastern Europe relative to those of France and have, thereby, sharply raised the scope for potential divergence in French and German policies there. Whatever the extent of harmonization of interests brought about in Western Europe through the open trade and open borders of the European Community, the influence of history, culture, and geography ensure that French and German interests and stakes in the East will differ. Without voluntaristic policy cooperation from Paris and Bonn, the structurally greater German interest in the East could force French and German foreign and security policies toward that region to diverge.

The predominant German interest in the East results from political, economic, and cultural factors. There are estimated to be, for example, more than 3 million ethnic Germans in the whole of Eastern Europe and the former Soviet Union, with more than 1 million in Russia, perhaps 400,000 in Poland, and 50,000 in Ukraine.[46] The political influence of these groups in Bonn is limited and declining but—if for no other reason than the fact that most of these Germans have the right to return to live in the Federal Republic—Germany cannot fail to take an interest in their well-being. Second, Germany—with an approximately 1,200 kilometer border with Poland and the Czech Republic—is also the recipient of most of Eastern Europe's refugees and immigrants, taking no less than 70 percent of all the asylum seekers of the entire EC during 1992.[47] For those fleeing poverty or chaos in the East, the destination is more likely to be the biggest, richest, and closest West European country than it is to be anywhere else. Third, even aside from security and immigration concerns, the German economic stake in the East is exceptional, at least when compared to that of Germany's European partners. As of mid-1993, German firms had provided 35 percent of total private investment in Eastern Europe and the former Soviet Union, and Germany was the largest trading partner of all the Central European states.[48] From 1989 to 1992, the Federal Republic also provided more than half the total international assistance to the republics of the former Soviet Union as well as more than half of total EC aid to Central and Eastern Europe.[49] Finally, German cultural links with the East are much greater than France's and are likely to grow. Though cultural ties and their importance are always difficult to measure, it is not irrelevant that German has become the leading foreign language in a number of East European countries and that more foreigners in Eastern Europe are learning German than anywhere else in the world.[50]

None of this is to say that France does not share some of these interests and that they can or will ignore what takes place east of the Oder river. But France's economic aid and investment, susceptibility to immigration, historical interest, and political ties with Eastern Europe are all considerably less than Germany's. France has no borders with East European countries; the number of its nationals in the region is insignificant; French private investment in Eastern Europe is considerably less than the German amount; and the French cultural role is limited to certain regions and elites. By contrast, France does have significant interests, relationships, and vulnerabilities in North Africa that are not shared by the Germans. Given these different political, economic, and strategic interests, it should not be surprising that, for the first several years after 1989, French and German approaches to ensuring security and stability in Eastern Europe significantly diverged.

France's initial approach to the new geopolitical situation that emerged from the revolutions of 1989 was—as suggested in the last section—to proceed quickly with the political and economic integration of Western Europe in order to bind the new Germany to the Community, to maintain the EC's cohesion, and to protect France's own leading role in Europe. On the surface at least, the French logic seemed impeccable: In a small, tight West European Community, France could dilute the new Germany's power and would remain at least one of two leaders, but in a broader and looser EC, Germany would become the Community's central and dominant state and German freedom of maneuver would increase. As an alternative to EC integration for the countries of Central and Eastern Europe, Mitterrand proposed a European "confederation"—to comprise all the states of the continent including Russia but not the United States—that would provide a forum for common pan-European political, economic, and technical discussions.[51]

The confederation plan was sharply rejected by the Central Europeans, the Americans, and (more politely) the Germans and most other West Europeans as well. The Americans, not surprisingly, did not like a plan that excluded them from European affairs and interpreted the plan as part of a longstanding French design to marginalize them from Europe. The Central Europeans, however, had the strongest objections: After 40 years of Soviet domination, they wanted no part of an organization that would include Russia but not the United States, and saw no reason that existing pan-European organizations [such as the Conference on Security and Cooperation in Europe (CSCE)] could not do the technical work proposed by the French. Even more important, the confederation gave Central Europeans the impression that it was no more than a second-class "waiting room" for states that would be excluded from the EC, a legitimate impression since Mitterrand announced on the radio in June 1991 that it would be "decades and decades" before they could join.[52] The confederation plan was rejected by the East Europeans at a June 1991 meeting in Prague, though it was not given up by the French, who insisted that the problem was mainly one of presentation and timing.[53]

The initial German strategy toward the East was not only philosophically different from France's but it was a much higher priority. More vulnerable to instability and the consequences of poverty or chaos, Germany became a strong advocate of massive Western assistance to former Communist states and a champion of their rapid integration into Western institutions. In contrast to Mitterrand's warnings about how long it would take to incorporate East European states into the EC, Kohl urged the Community to act quickly on new memberships and argued that the stabilization of "the political, economic, and social conditions in Central and southeastern Europe as well as in the [former] Soviet Union" were needed "more than anything else."[54] Germany was also in the forefront of Western efforts to extend NATO's institutional links with the East and played a leading role in the creation of the North Atlantic Cooperation Council (NACC), a forum that brings together the states of NATO and the former Warsaw pact, which French officials initially rejected as unnecessary, redundant, and potentially misleading to East Europeans in search of military guarantees.[55] During late 1991 and 1992, France came to accept the NACC, took a more liberal attitude toward the eventual EC membership of Central European states, and grudgingly accepted an opening of EC markets for exports from Central Europe to which they had initially been opposed.[56] Nonetheless, despite longstanding claims of wanting to "surpass Yalta," France under the Socialists seemed less prepared than Germany to extend either extensive Western aid or Western institutions to the countries of the East.

There has been some limited convergence of French and German positions on Eastern Europe since the March 1993 election of the center-right government of Edouard Balladur. The Balladur government came to power after criticizing the Socialists for their "backwardness" in adapting to change in Eastern Europe and after accusing Mitterrand of maintaining out-of-date "Cold War" views.[57] Skeptical about the Socialists' plans for West European federal integration, the Rally for the Republic (RPR)—the leading party in the governing coalition—called for a more rapid integration into the community of the Central European states, and Balladur himself spoke in favor of their integration into NATO.[58] In the late summer of 1993, Defense Minister François Léotard traveled throughout Central Europe to discuss security and even concluded limited agreements with the states of the region on topics such as the formation of peacekeeping units with the Czech Republic.[59] Most concretely, in mid-1993 the Balladur government put forth a plan for a European "pact for stability and security in Europe" that would guarantee borders throughout Europe, protect minorities within states, provide a security forum in which all Europeans could participate, and, it is hoped in Paris, compensate for Europe's failures in meeting any of these goals during the Yugoslav crisis. The Balladur plan was presented to the European Council in Copenhagen in June 1993 and adopted as part of the Common Foreign and Security Policy by the European Council in the Brussels summit of December 11-12, 1993.[60] Like Mitterrand's "confederation," this new French plan is a way—short of full membership in the EC and NATO—to extend an institutional hand to the East Europeans, while excluding the Central Asians and (this time) including the United States.

Some Germans welcomed this new French initiative and saw it as a sign of France "finally coming around" on Eastern Europe and showing a willingness to engage there.[61] Most others, however, were highly skeptical and privately criticized the security pact as one more instance in a long line of French diversions, excuses to stop short of what was really necessary. In fact, it is legitimate to wonder why Europe needed yet another treaty and why guaranteed borders and protection for minorities are not adequately provided for in the 1975 Helsinki Final Act or by the United Nations. Even more pertinently, one can ask whether any European proclamations of support for existing borders or minority rights would be credible in the immediate aftermath of the failure to do either in former Yugoslavia. The Balladur "security pact" may show a growing French recognition of the all-European interest in security in the East, but it provides little objective support for security there and risks appearing to Central Europeans already disappointed in the French level of engagement as little more than a symbolic gesture.

An even more pressing security issue for France, Germany, and the alliance where Eastern Europe is concerned has been that of full NATO and WEU membership for the Central European states, an issue that took on great prominence in the weeks before the January 10-11, 1994, NATO summit in Brussels. Longing for security guarantees and dissatisfied with the NACC, the Central European states all made it known before the summit— more loudly than ever after the December 1993 electoral success of Russian extreme nationalist Vladimir Zhirinovsky—that they wanted to become full members of Western security alliances in the near future.[62] Although the policymaking communities in France, Germany, and other allied states were all divided on the issue, there were signs during 1993 to 1994 that the German willingness to welcome the East into formerly Western alliances would exceed that of the others. Already in March 1993, German defense minister Volker Rühe began to express his concern about a "strategic vacuum" opening up on Germany's eastern border and to call for the alliance to consider extending guarantees to the countries of Central Europe.[63] Five months later, Foreign Minister Klaus Kinkel called for the alliance to work toward enlargement by involving the Central European states in NATO peacekeeping and peacemaking activities through the NACC. Kinkel also proposed— picking up an issue that had been supported by CDU foreign policy spokesman Karl Lamers—that the WEU offer association status to all candidates for membership in the EC, including Central European countries, and that NATO declare its willingness to make bilateral agreements on security cooperation with all countries seeking membership in the EC.[64] The German foreign office tended to be more reticent about expansion than the defense ministry, and German officials at NATO warned that an expanded NATO would "be a very different NATO."[65] But as 1994 began there was real momentum in Germany toward support for an eventual full inclusion of the Central European states in both the European and Atlantic alliances.

In the run-up to the summit, France, the United States, and other NATO members also expressed a willingness to consider the issue of full alliance expansion to Central Europe, but none went as far as Germany. French defense minister François Léotard maintained that the entrance of Central European states in NATO was not "immediately possible" and suggested that France would prefer to welcome them "in the two forums of consultation of the Western European Union and the North Atlantic Cooperation Council."[66] Léotard also warned against a premature entrance of new states in the WEU on the grounds that this West European forum should first be built up and strengthened before it is diluted with any new members.[67] There was similar reticence in the United States, where, despite strong support from some leading senators and growing momentum in the foreign policy communities, many were skeptical about extending new guarantees abroad at a time when most Americans want to focus more attention on problems at home.[68] While the Clinton administration made great efforts during the week before the Brussels summit to reassure the Central Europeans (Clinton sent top advisers to the region and even proposed "war games" with Poland), at the summit the United States remained unprepared to offer a concrete timetable for full Central European membership in NATO. The alternative—a plan called Partnership for Peace that offered security consultations and expanded military cooperation—put off the issue for the time being but did not resolve it.[69]

In the months following the NATO summit, both France and Germany sought to dispel the impression that Central Europe was being slighted (or that French and German policies were out of sync) and announced plans for a joint *"Ostpolitik"* to be implemented during their successive presidencies of the European Union in 1994 and 1995.[70] But however sincere the two countries' pledges to coordinate their future Eastern strategies, it could not be hidden that it was mainly German leaders who were demanding the rapid integration of Central European states into the EU, and it was not clear that French leaders shared Chancellor Kohl's view that it was "unthinkable" that Germany's border with Poland "should remain the eastern border of the European Union."[71] What the French did believe was that "everything must be done to prevent the reemergence of a partition of Europe and of a logic of blocs, whose borders would merely have been shifted in comparison with the Cold War period."[72] A quarrel that emerged when the French ambassador in Bonn criticized the German foreign minister for dominating the EU-entry negotiations with the Scandinavian countries and Austria was perhaps only a foreshadowing of Franco-German disputes to come.[73] No matter how hard they try, France and Germany cannot change the fact that their national interests in Central and Eastern Europe do not always coincide.

Could divergent interests and perspectives on Eastern Europe lead to splits between Germany and France or between Germany and the rest of the alliance? It is important not to exaggerate this potential. The new Germany may have long borders with the East—but it continues to have longer ones with the West. It may have the opportunity to revive old, cultural and historical links in the East—but none of these ever rivaled the depth of the Federal Republic's relations with the West for the past forty years. Perhaps most important, Eastern Europe's share of German external trade might be growing from its present 5-6 percent, but the EU continues to take more than half (53 percent) of overall German trade. France's share of total German trade is 12 percent, whereas Poland's share, for example, is barely 1 percent.[74] The countries of the present European and Atlantic communities remain Germany's main area of foreign policy interest, and it would clearly be folly for Bonn to put that relationship at risk for potential gains in the East.

Keeping that in mind, it remains true that relative to the Cold War period, German political, security and economic interests in the East have grown substantially as well as disproportionately to those of France and other Western states. Germany will seek to involve France and the rest of the West in its Eastern zone of interest and to co-opt French assistance in stabilizing this critical region. To the extent that Western Europe continues to integrate, French and German interests will continue to converge. But if France and others fail to respond to German particular interests in the East, Germany will be obliged to take action itself. It seems a fundamental challenge for France and the other allies not to let Eastern Europe become a domain of exclusive German responsibility.

War and Diplomacy in Former Yugoslavia

For the purposes of this study, the most pertinent question about France and Germany in Yugoslavia is not so much why they failed to prevent the war—that would be too demanding an expectation—but why they failed even to pursue common policies toward it. Why, for example, after thirty years of seeking—as the Elysée Treaty put it—to develop "common conceptions" and strategies, did Germany and France fail to do so in such a critical area? Are divergent interests and perspectives in Central Europe stronger than the will to cooperate nurtured for more than forty years? Is the failure to pursue common policies in Yugoslavia an exceptional situation, or is it portentous of things to come? These questions can obviously not be answered definitively here, but an analysis of French and German policies toward the war in former Yugoslavia does shed light on the broader Franco-German relationship and its potential role in Western security.

Divergence between France and Germany over how to interpret and what to do about Yugoslavia was apparent from the very beginning of the conflict. Whereas France saw the conflict primarily as an internal affair to be resolved by continued negotiation among the Yugoslav republics, Germany emphasized the right of peoples to self-determination and sympathized with the desires of the northern republics of Slovenia and Croatia for independence. These diverging analyses led to differing policies toward the early stages of the war that broke out between Slovenia and the central Yugoslav government in June 1991: Whereas France continued throughout the summer and fall to insist on the maintenance of the Yugoslav federation, Germany began to push for the recognition of Slovenia and Croatia, a policy preference announced by Foreign Minister Genscher as early as September 1991.[75] Throughout the autumn, France and Germany tried to harmonize their policies bilaterally and within the European Community and even put forth a joint proposal for a European buffer force in September 1991, but that project never materialized. The Germans themselves felt unable to participate for historical and constitutional reasons, and the United States and United Kingdom were intent on trying to keep the Yugoslav federation intact and were unwilling to countenance the deployment of military forces to the region.[76] Not for the first time—both because of internal divergences and lack of support by the Western allies—the Franco-German partnership showed its limits as an actor in international security.

After months of unsuccessful EC efforts to mediate the conflict diplomatically, German patience expired and German chancellor Kohl declared in early December 1991 that Germany would recognize Slovenia and Croatia "by Christmas," a promise extended to the German public as well as the Croatian and Slovenian leaders.[77] A week later, after long and tense negotiations between supporters and opponents of recognition, the EC announced a compromise plan to recognize only those Yugoslav republics meeting certain conditions by January 15, 1992. Germany, however, made it clear that it did not feel bound by the conditions and recognized Slovenia and Croatia on December 23, 1991, followed reluctantly by France and the rest of the EC several weeks later.[78] Some German and EC leaders sought to present their recognition policy as a common action based on a broad consensus reached by the twelve EC states, but the reality seems to be that French, German, and other allied analyses and prescriptions were dissimilar and that "joint" recognition resulted more from an effort to harmonize Community policy than from fundamental agreement on the policy itself.[79] Some observers have even suggested that the common agreement to recognize on January 15 was the result of an implicit or explicit "deal" between Germany and France: The former accepted European monetary union as a quid pro quo for the latter's acceptance of recognition.[80]

Why, though, did German, French, and other analyses and policies differ? Why did it prove so difficult for the Western allies to reach agreement not only on what was happening in Yugoslavia but, more importantly, on what to do about it? The answers have to do with a broad combination of historical, geographical, cultural, and political factors whose relative weight is difficult, but important, to assess for both Germany and France.

Active German support for the recognition of Croatia and Slovenia resulted from all of the following factors in varying degrees.

Domestic Political Pressures

From the very beginning of the conflict in former Yugoslavia, the German government came under intense domestic and media pressure to "do something" to stop the war and destruction.[81] An active press campaign led by the editorialists of the *Frankfurter Allgemeine Zeitung* and *Die Welt* as well as German television reports contributed to the increased pressure on German leaders to act in some way. The German media portrayed the conflict in former Yugoslavia as largely a one-sided Serbian/Communist oppression of innocent Croats and Slovenes; it reported little of the problems of the Serbian minority in Croatia or other unflattering aspects of the potential Croatian regime. In addition, the Roman Catholic Church in Germany, with strong ties to its branches in Slovenia and Croatia and its influence on the Christian Democrats and especially the Bavarian Christian Social Union, was very active in pushing for recognition of the breakaway republics.[82] A large Yugoslavian immigrant community, nearly two-thirds of whose 700,000 members were Croatian and whose church representative had long been active in cultural affairs in Germany, added to pressures for recognition of and sympathy for Croatia.[83] By the end of the summer of 1991, even secular SPD leaders were on the bandwagon of recognition, creating a broad political-social consensus in the country that Genscher and other leaders in Bonn ultimately could not resist.[84]

Support for the Notion of "Self-determination"

Numerous German leaders perceived an obligation to recognize Slovenia and Croatia not only as an attempt to stop the war but also as a result of their belief in the principle of self-determination.[85] Germans, after all, had just experienced reunification based on the self-determination of those who lived in the East and as a nation had just celebrated their own victory over foreign oppression and communism; they could not easily deny the same right to other deserving peoples. Then-CDU chairman Volker Rühe explained it this way in July 1991: "We won our unity through the right to self-determination. If we Germans think everything else in Europe can stay just as it was, if we follow a status quo policy and do not recognize the right to self-determination in Slovenia and Croatia, then we have no moral or political credibility."[86] The German concept of self-determination was fueled, moreover, by a conception of nationhood based more on ethnic origin (*jus sanguinis*) than territory (*jus soli*), which made it logical for Germans to support self-determination for the Croat and Slovene "nations." Finally, the fact that Germany, unlike some of its West European partners, is not itself beset with potential breakaway regions or republics perhaps made German opinion less sensitive than others to the inherent problems of the notion of self-determination.[87]

Faith in International Law

The German emphasis on recognition as a tool to stop the fighting seems to reflect an emphasis on legal aspects of international questions and faith in international law that has long been a characteristic of German foreign policy.[88] Specifically, German leaders, caught up in the heady spirit of the early post-unification period, seemed to believe that international norms and institutions could contribute to the prevention of further conflict in northern Yugoslavia and that the Serbian forces attacking Croatia might hesitate to do so if the problem were "internationalized" in law. As Genscher explained it already in an August 1991 interview in *Die Zeit*, "recognition" would be an alternative to "accepting a policy of border changes by force while standing idly by."[89] Without a military option available, the German logic that recognition would prevent further war or aggression was inevitably based on the assumption or hope that newly recognized international borders would be respected.[90]

Proximity to the Conflict

An obvious stimulus to Germany's willingness to act decisively and even unilaterally in Yugoslavia was Germany's proximity to the conflict and fears of the impact of refugees fleeing war adding to the already growing number of asylum seekers in the Federal Republic. As the largest and richest country in the region, with a large Yugoslav community and a tradition of liberal asylum policies, Germany would surely be the target of most of those fleeing Yugoslavia. Such factors, together with the traditional German passion for stability after the experiences of the early 20th century, probably explain Germany's relatively strong initial involvement better than any post-unification desires for a superpower-like role. Nonetheless, the great successes of unification and German confidence in their knowledge of the Balkans and Eastern Europe may well have contributed to a certain "hubris" on the part of those who believed that Germany was best placed to take the lead in the Yugoslav conflict.[91]

Geopolitical Considerations

Contrary to some suspicions held at the time, Germany was not out to build some sort of "Teutonic bloc" by recognizing Croatia and Slovenia. Genuine compassion for victims of aggression and a belief—perhaps naive—that recognition could help stop that aggression were probably more important factors than calculations of national interest. Having said that, the creation in Central Europe of two potential protégés with linguistic, religious, and historical ties to Germany could hardly be seen with displeasure in Bonn. It would be wrong to attribute primary importance to geopolitical considerations in Germany's recognition of Slovenia and Croatia but it should be recognized that they existed. It is perhaps worth noting that Austria and Switzerland, the two other German-speaking states of the region, were strongly behind early recognition of Slovenia and Croatia.

In the case of France, the following factors seem to be most important in bringing about resistance to recognition of the Yugoslav republics.

The French Conception of the Nation-state

As a highly centralized state formed through the assimilation of diverse regions and peoples over the centuries, France tended to see Yugoslavia not as a collection of distinct peoples but as a unit to be held together through integration. While obviously not unaware of the diverging aspirations of the various members of the Yugoslav federation, France nonetheless emphasized the principle of maintaining existing borders more than that of an inherent right to self-determination, which, France believed, was highly problematic in a region like the Balkans. If the Francs, Bretons, Alsacians, and Basques could be united and assimilated into a centralized republic, why could the Serbs, Croats, and Moslems not at least find some sort of *modus vivendi*? With sometimes violent separatist problems of its own, moreover—particularly in Corsica—France was also concerned that an acceptance of a general trend toward "self-determination" could threaten France's own national and territorial unity.

Fears About Implications for Eastern Europe and the Soviet Union

Like other states that opposed recognition, France based its arguments largely on the precedent that recognition would set for Eastern Europe and the former Soviet Union, where a myriad of potential border disputes could erupt if ethnic groups were led to believe that each had the right to an independent state. Speaking in September 1991, Mitterrand warned about the perils of applying self-determination elsewhere in Eastern Europe: "I have determined seventeen similar situations, and I am expecting many more. . . . Yesterday there were thirty-three states—and tomorrow? The right of self-determination is not to be questioned. But let us make sure that it is exercised in a democratic way and in conjunction with the treaties that guarantee security and peace on our continent."[92] These fears obviously existed in Germany as well—Bonn, for example, did not announce its intention to recognize Slovenia and Croatia until *after* the Soviet breakup had become clear—but were outweighed by other considerations. With fewer incentives than Germany for seeing the northern republics become independent, France preferred the injustices of a federation dominated from Belgrade by force to a breakup that could lead to civil war elsewhere in Eastern Europe.

"Containment" of German Influence

It seems likely, although it cannot easily be demonstrated, that one factor influencing French policy in the Balkans was a desire to contain the continued expansion of German influence in Central Europe. Just as France sought during the winter of 1989-1990 to prevent or delay German unification before finally accepting it, in Yugoslavia France first tried to oppose German actions before reluctantly accepting them. To use terms common in international relations theory, France first tried to "balance" its larger neighbor, and when that did not work it sought to "bandwagon" with it.[93] This is not to say that France consciously feared that Germany was considering detaching itself from its Western ties in favor of putative new ones in the East—even the French knew this to be unlikely—but to state the obvious point that France had less of an interest in seeing the independence of two new German-oriented states in the wake of German unification. French foreign policy has often been driven by a concern about Germany (the reaction to *Ostpolitik* in the early 1970s and the rapprochement with NATO in the early 1980s are just two examples), and French policy in Yugoslavia seems no exception: A Serbian-led federation, at least, had the merit of being unlikely to fall into Germany's growing "orbit."[94]

Historical Relations with Serbia

To interpret French policy toward Yugoslavia primarily as the result of a strong "pro-Serb" bias and nostalgia for an old wartime ally is to misunderstand French knowledge and views about that Balkan state. Until 1991, much of the French public did not differentiate at all between the various Yugoslav republics or ethnic groups, and the factors already mentioned were clearly much more important to French policy than attitudes toward the Serbs. Still, one can conclude that historical memories may have influenced French policy to a certain degree. Whatever the views of the French public, President Mitterrand and Foreign Minister Dumas happened to be of the wartime generation, and it cannot be excluded that their analyses were influenced by historical memories—of Serb allies and Croatian Ustasha (allies of the Nazis during World War II)—that would not have affected younger men. French leaders, in any case, on a number of occasions referred to their historic ties with Serbia, and as late as the summer of 1992 Mitterrand was still making clear that he had "not forgotten the historic ties between France and Serbia and the solidarity that bound them together in two world wars."[95] There was, in any case, more reporting in France than in Germany of the problems faced by minorities in Croatia as well as those in Serbia.[96] Since the change of government in March 1993, France has been led by leaders probably too young to share such memories and who, perhaps for more than domestic political reasons, have criticized Mitterrand and Dumas's "pro-Serbian" bias.[97]

In other important alliance countries, domestic, cultural, and economic factors also played important roles in determining policy toward Yugoslavia. The United States, having just fought a major war in the Persian Gulf, was distracted from events taking place in the Balkans and was hardly inclined to become engaged there when vital U.S. national interests did not appear to be at stake. The U.S. military had learned certain "lessons" from its experience in Vietnam, and one of those was to stay out of conflicts that cannot be handled with decisive military force applied toward a clear and definable objective. American leaders were also concerned about the precedent a breakup of Yugoslavia would set for the Soviet Union, and with a presidential election coming up, an early U.S. decision was taken "not to lose one American life in Yugoslavia."[98] The United Kingdom's reticence toward recognition of or engagement in Yugoslav republics was similar to that of the Americans, and was augmented by Britain's own experiences in Northern Ireland and a historic British view that the Balkans were somehow "different" from the rest of Europe.[99] The British seemed to have the best sense of all—some might argue it was a self-fulfilling prophesy—that the West would never intervene militarily on behalf of the new republics, and, therefore, that recognition should be withheld. British foreign secretary Douglas Hurd put it rather presciently in a December 1991 article in *The London Times*:

> Recognition will not stop the fighting. Nor will the West send troops to fight on Croatia's behalf. If we recognize the republics too soon, we risk detonating the fragile peace in Macedonia and Bosnia, since they will come under great pressure to seek independence too. Recognition

of a series of small Balkan countries, without a framework allowing for cooperation and protection of minorities, would not be a recipe for future stability."[100]

Both of the "Anglo-Saxon" countries, in any case, were doubtless influenced by the fact that they were far removed from the conflict and would therefore be least affected by turmoil there. In the end, whatever the particular reasons for individual Western policies toward recognition, the policy result combined the worst of all possible worlds. New borders were brought about and recognized without any guarantees that those new borders would be protected (by military force if need be), and new countries were created that did not give any assurance that they would respect the conditions on human rights, minorities, and borders that the European Community had demanded. With recognition granted only to Slovenia and Croatia, moreover, the Bosnian republic was forced to choose between an inviable independence and continued membership in a Yugoslavia now all the more dominated by the former Communists and Serbs ruling in Belgrade. Unwilling to accept the latter arrangement, Bosnia's Moslem-led government chose in March 1992 the independence that quickly led to a devastating war.[101]

The Western disagreements over recognition of the former Yugoslav republics left traces in the alliance and were the source of mutual recriminations among France, Germany, Great Britain, and the United States. In January 1993, President Mitterrand explained that he considered early recognition of Croatia and Slovenia to be a "major error," and suggested (without naming Germany) that Bonn was largely responsible for what had taken place.[102] Mitterrand's foreign minister Roland Dumas spoke in June 1993 of the "decisive responsibilities" of the Germans and the Catholic Church for the "acceleration of the crisis," and other French leaders such as Laurent Fabius also suggested recognition was a mistake.[103] Most controversially, U.S. Secretary of State Warren Christopher claimed in June 1993 that Germany bore "particular responsibility" for the "serious mistakes made in the whole process of recognition," echoing suggestions made a few months earlier by former UN mediator Cyrus Vance that recognition was "premature" and had "brought about the war that is now going on."[104] German leaders have expressed dismay about all these implicit or explicit accusations and have responded that recognition was inevitable, agreed by unanimity among the Twelve, and not premature but rather too late: Blaming Germany, they argued, was simply a convenient and irresponsible excuse for the failure of Western policy in general.[105]

After the divergences in the winter of 1991-1992, French and German policies toward former Yugoslavia began—in some ways—to converge. With recognition of the former Yugoslav republics now a *fait accompli*, the French preference for maintaining a unified state was no longer an option, and Paris was forced to take account of the new situation. In addition, increasingly flagrant Serbian aggression made it impossible for France to maintain the line that Serbia should not be isolated. In May 1992, the French government agreed after a long delay to support the imposition of UN economic sanctions against Serbia and Montenegro and took an increasingly tough line against the Belgrade regime.[106]

Germany's position during 1992 also changed but for different reasons. Normally quite cautious about acting in a multilateral context and not used to taking the lead on security matters beyond its own borders, German leaders were surprised and taken aback by the vehemence of the international reaction to recognition. Talk of a new "German assertiveness" in Washington and fears of German domination of Europe expressed sharply elsewhere reminded the always image-conscious Germans that their foreign policy actions—even (or especially) after unification—would continue to be scrutinized carefully by their allies.[107] By the spring of 1992—when the raging war in Bosnia made it obvious that recognition would not have the desired effect—Germany began to take a more reserved role in the conflict and to seek even more than before to coordinate its policies with those of France and the other allies. Foreign Minister Kinkel stated that Germans, "with our constitutional problems and our historic burden, are the last ones who should be giving . . . suggestions in this matter" and Defense Minister Rühe announced that Germany should be "particularly reserved when it comes to advice" because of its limited possibilities.[108]

Yet if both France and Germany now saw the conflict in more similar and balanced terms, their roles in that conflict remained significantly different, largely because of the respective military and diplomatic roles each was willing or able to play. France was not only a permanent UN Security Council member and thus co-responsible for many of the main international decisions taken by the international community, but it was also the country supplying the largest number of peacekeeping troops to the region as well as the overall commander of UN troops there. France played a prominent role in enforcing the 1991 NATO/WEU naval embargo on Yugoslavia, agreed by the end of 1992 to take a full part in the military enforcement of a no-fly zone over Yugoslavia, participated in Western air drops of humanitarian aid to Bosnian towns in March 1993, and in May put forth a five-country plan to create and defend militarily "security zones" for

Moslems in isolated pockets in Bosnia.[109] France was also instrumental in the organization and implementation of NATO's February 10, 1994, ultimatum demanding the withdrawal of Serb artillery from the Sarajevo area. France's leading military role in former Yugoslavia should not be exaggerated—it was hardly a full-fledged military intervention—but compared to many of France's allies, including Germany, the French role did stand out— a point that French leaders did not hesitate to stress.[110]

Germany's military role in former Yugoslavia was necessarily more limited. By the end of 1993, of course, the German military had taken unprecedented steps, including numerous deliveries of humanitarian relief by military transport to Sarajevo and other parts of Bosnia; sending a destroyer to the Adriatic Sea as part of a WEU mission to observe implementation of an embargo against Serbia; executing air drops of humanitarian relief to isolated populations in eastern Bosnia; and playing a leading role in NATO AWACS force involved in implementing first the sanctions, against Yugoslavia and later the no-fly zone whose enforcement was declared in January 1993. These measures all showed an increasing German willingness to take on responsibilities for international security and a growing readiness to participate even in the military aspects of peacekeeping, sanctions and humanitarian aid.

At the same time, however, the use of international military forces in Yugoslavia made clear just how limited Germany's role was and how limited, therefore, were the prospects of active Franco-German military cooperation. German troop deployments, as part of a peacekeeping force on the French or British model, were ruled out from the start for "historical reasons."[111] The Adriatic deployment was part only of a monitoring force with no military mission (indeed, the ship's guns were reportedly spiked), and even so the opposition SPD took the government to court in order to try to stop the mission.[112] Similarly, there was strong domestic political opposition to German participation in NATO's AWACS force even though German officers would take no part in any eventual combat but would only direct or guide potential Western air operations; it took a constitutional court decision to allow German pilots to participate.[113] A telling symbol of Germany's reduced diplomatic role (partly as a consequence of its military limitations) was the five-country "Washington Plan" on Bosnia mentioned above: The countries involved were the United States, France, Russia, Great Britain, and Spain—but not Germany.[114] Because of all these constraints, one is obliged to conclude that the obstacles to Franco-German military cooperation in former Yugoslavia were no less--indeed they were even greater—than the obstacles to political cooperation. The impact of the two main Franco-German military proposals—the September 1991 call for a buffer force to be sent to Croatia and the April 1992 joint plan to send a UN peace mission to Bosnia-Hercegovina—were limited by the fact that Germany would not have participated in them and were, as one analyst has concluded, probably "directed more at patching up differences between the two countries than at finding solutions to the crisis."[115] As in the Gulf War, constraints on Germany's use of military force and France's desire to play a prominent national role—along with differing geopolitical and historical perspectives in the two countries—reduced the scope for effective Franco-German military cooperation. In this particular domain, French policies were more similar to and more in harmony with British policies than with German ones.

The very fact of French and British but not German or American engagement on the ground led to further policy differences among the European and North American allies, notably their positions on maintaining the arms embargo on the Bosnian Moslems and the use of NATO or American airstrikes against Serbian positions. Beginning in early 1993, President Clinton began to call for the arms embargo to be lifted and for NATO to make air strikes against Serbian positions as deterrents to further "ethnic cleansing." Germany, still seeking to do something for the victims of aggression and anxious to involve the United States, showed increasing support for the American position during the spring and by June 1993 had agreed to encourage its European partners to lift the arms embargo against the Moslems.[116] France and Great Britain, however—concerned about their peacekeepers on the ground and fearful that lifting the embargo or making NATO airstrikes would only prolong the fighting—forcefully opposed the American plan.[117] A trip to European capitals by U.S. secretary of state Warren Christopher in May 1993 failed to convince the Europeans to adopt the American approach, and Christopher returned home empty handed, announcing that "our allies have particular ideas of their own that they want to pursue at the present time."[118] In an unprecedented (and perhaps portentous) show of allied resistance to a U.S. proposal, Britain and France formally opposed the American plan at the UN Security Council in June 1993.[119] The recriminations that had first surfaced over recognition now reappeared in the form of sometimes bitter transatlantic debates over who was most to blame for failing to stop the war.[120]

As 1994 began there were signs that some of the Western actors in the Yugoslav conflict were beginning to harmonize their policies and that more active American and NATO involvement in the war might have some effect. France, frustrated with the failures of the UN mediation efforts and increasingly unable to support what seemed like an indefinite deployment of peacekeepers to the Balkans, began in late 1993 to press for more active American involvement in the region and succeeded at the January 1994 NATO summit in getting the United States to threaten the use of military force for certain specific purposes: to lift the siege of Sarajevo, open the airport in Tuzla, and allow the relief of a Canadian battalion holed up in the central Bosnian town of Srebrenica.[121] In February 1994, France and the United States teamed up yet again to organize a joint response to the shelling of a Sarajevo market that had killed dozens of civilians, and the NATO ultimatum that resulted on February 10—demanding that all Serb artillery within 20 kilometers of Sarajevo be withdrawn or put under UN control within 10 days—seemed to infuse new momentum into the putative peace process.[122] During the weeks that followed, the Serbs complied with NATO's demands, Sarajevans began to circulate throughout their city, and Croats and Muslims agreed to merge their two parts of Bosnia and form a confederation with Croatia, leading some observers to express cautious hope that two-and-a-half years of Balkan savagery and Western disunity were finally coming to an end.[123] No one should overlook, however, the enormous potential for conflict that presently remains in former Yugoslavia, and even in the unlikely event that the hopes of mid-1994 are ultimately fulfilled, it will be difficult for the European and transatlantic allies to claim that their unity, solidarity, or engagement had very much to do with the result.

Former Yugoslavia's problems stem from deep-seated fears and insecurities among its member populations, and those populations are so deeply interspersed that conflict among them may have been inevitable once these insecurities got out of hand.[124] It is, thus, by no means clear that more coherent or unified Western policies could have had a decisive effect on events in Yugoslavia and it may well be that the tragedy there would have developed along largely similar lines regardless of what the West had done. But the case can also be made that a decisive and common Western policy— *either* to recognize breakaway Yugoslavian republics and to defend them with military force *or* to refuse recognition until certain conditions were met; *either* to protect the Moslems with arms and military support *or* to make it clear to them from the start that they would get no military assistance; *either* to use military force for peacekeeping only *or* to threaten or use air strikes against aggressors—would have been better than the compromises, half-measures, contradictions, and misleading promises that resulted from Western divisions. At the very least, Western disagreements over Yugoslavia demonstrated a lamentable lack of agreement on a central security issue that portends badly for European or transatlantic cohesion in the post-Cold War world. It can only be seen as bitterly ironic that the announcement of the European Community's "common foreign and security policy" began with this manifest demonstration of the lack of unity among its most important members.

From these failures, several tentative conclusions can be drawn, none of which is very encouraging for Franco-German, European, or transatlantic cooperation. First, French, German, and other Western policies and views toward the conflict in Yugoslavia resulted primarily from *national* histories, cultures, geography, and interests. The conflict was perceived through national lenses and interpreted by national media. Despite years of supposed harmonization of West European perspectives and interests through the EC, France, Germany, and Great Britain still had diverging national interests and perspectives toward the republics of former Yugoslavia. One can hope that the case of Yugoslavia was an exception and that continued Western integration and greater efforts to coordinate foreign policy will lead to greater similarity in the analyses of potential future conflicts; but one must admit that in this case such unity did not exist.

Second, just as in the war in the Persian Gulf, the role of Franco-German security cooperation was extremely limited in Yugoslavia. Despite the various Franco-German defense and security councils and commissions and the regular meetings of senior officials and politicians, French and German policies toward former Yugoslavia resulted from national assessments more than from joint ones. Diplomats worked primarily in national channels and sought to coordinate national positions once those positions had been formed and articulated by political leaders, not beforehand as would be necessary if a truly common assessment or policy were to be made. To the extent that Western countries played a role in Yugoslavia, it was carried out through the UN Security Council (where France was a member and Germany was not), NATO (where the United States was dominant), the European Community (limited to diplomatic measures), or individually as nation-states. A specifically "Franco-German" role was almost totally absent in Yugoslavia, and Franco-German coordination was no better (and was sometimes worse) than French or German cooperation with other allies, depending on the issue.

Finally, the lack of Franco-German and broader European unity in Yugoslavia reveals a more serious, structural problem with European security after the Cold War: Europe no longer has a "natural" leader like the United States. Germany is the only country potentially in a position to play a leadership role but it is not prepared to do so and its neighbors are not ready to accept such a role. Pluralism will be a more difficult arrangement than hegemony, whatever the drawbacks of the latter. If the Western alliance wants to have a more unified foreign policy in the post-Cold War era, either the United States must continue to lead it—which seems unlikely given America's domestic priorities—or France and Germany are going to have to find a way jointly to provide political will and means to the European Community. If they fail to do that, Yugoslavia will prove to be more the rule than the exception.

Notes

[1] On the motivations of Franco-German cooperation in the postwar period, see F. Roy Willis, *France, Germany and the New Europe: 1945-67*, rev. ed., (London: Oxford University Press, 1968); Edwina S. Campbell, *Germany's Past & Europe's Future: The Challenges of West German Foreign Policy* (Washington DC: Pergamon-Brassey's, 1989), especially chaps. 3-4; and Julius W. Friend, *The Linchpin: French-German Relations, 1950-1990*, The Washington Papers, no. 154 (Washington, DC: Praeger/Center for Strategic and International Studies, 1991).

[2] See Stanley Hoffmann, "La France dans le nouvel ordre européen," *Politique étrangère* (fall 1990):504.

[3] For a compelling analysis of the perils of the post-Cold War world, see Pierre Lellouche, *Le nouveau monde: De l'ordre de Yalta au désordre des nations* (Paris: Grasset, 1992).

[4] For pessimistic assessments of the prospects for post-Cold War Franco-German relations and Western European cooperation more generally, see Alain Minc, *La grande illusion* (Paris: Grasset, 1989); Georges Valence, *France-Allemagne: Le Retour de Bismarck* (Paris: Flammarion, 1990); John J. Mearsheimer, "Back to the Future: Instability in Europe after the Cold War," *International Security* 15, no. 1 (summer 1990):5-56; and Conor Cruise O'Brien, "The Future of the West," *The National Interest* (winter 1992-1993):3-10. The classic formulation of the "neorealist" argument that international structures primarily determine national behavior is Kenneth N. Waltz, *Theory of International Politics* (Reading, MA: Addison-Wesley, 1979). For some critiques, see Robert O. Keohane, *Neorealism and its Critics* (New York: Columbia University Press, 1986).

[5] For the prediction of nostalgia for the Cold War, see John J. Mearsheimer, "Why We Will Soon Miss the Cold War," *Atlantic Monthly* 266 (August 1990): 35-37.

[6] For arguments about the importance played by *rang* in France's Gulf policy, see François Heisbourg, "France and the Gulf Crisis," in Nicole Gnesotto and John Roper, eds., *Western Europe and the Gulf* (Paris: Institute for Security Studies, Western European Union, 1992), pp. 17-38; David S. Yost, "France and the Per-

sian Gulf War of 1990-1991: Political-Military Lessons Learned," *Journal of Strategic Studies* 16, no. 3 (September 1993):339-74; and Philip H. Gordon, *French Security Policy after the Cold War: Continuity, Change and Implications for the United States*, R-4229-A (Santa Monica, CA: RAND, 1992), pp. 33-42.

[7] See "Le 'rang' de la France," *Le Monde*, March 5, 1991; and André Fontaine, "Retrouver l'Europe," *Le Monde*, March 8, 1991.

[8] Whereas article 24 of the German Basic Law allows Germany to participate in international collective security organizations, article 87 (2) prohibits the use of the Bundeswehr for any actions that are not "specifically permitted by the constitution." Since 1982, German leaders have concluded—wrongly according to many constitutional scholars—that this prohibits the use of German military forces beyond NATO's zone. On the decision in Bonn that this prohibition would hold for the Gulf, see Karl Kaiser and Klaus Becher, *Deutschland und der Irak-Konflikt: Internationale Sicherheitsverantwortung Deutschlands und Europas nach der deutschen Vereinigung*, Arbeitspapiere zur Internationalen Politik 68 (Bonn: Forschungsinstitut der Deutschen Gesellschaft für Auswärtige Politik, February 1992), p. 15. For a shorter, English version of the study, see Karl Kaiser and Klaus Becher, "Germany and the Iraq conflict," in Gnesotto and Roper, eds., *Western Europe and the Gulf*, pp. 42-43.

[9] On Mitterrand's diplomatic initiatives during the Gulf War, see Roland Dannreuther, *The Gulf Conflict: A Political and Strategic Analysis*, Adelphi Paper 264 (London: International Institute for Strategic Studies, winter 1991/92), pp. 35-45; and Josette Alia and Christine Clerc, *La guerre de Mitterrand: La dernière illusion* (Paris: Olivier Orbin, 1991).

[10] On the military dimension of Germany's role, see Thomas Enders and Michael J. Inacker, "The Second Gulf War and Germany: Contributions and Political and Military Lessons," unpublished paper presented to the Center for National Security Studies's study of foreign perspectives on the Gulf War, paper provided by Center for National Security Studies, Los Alamos National Laboratory, 1992; as well as Kaiser and Becher, *Deutschland und der Irak-Konflikt*.

[11] See Kaiser and Becher, *Deutschland und der Irak-Konflikt*, pp. 47-52.

[12] See Major quoted in *The Times* (London), January 22, 1991. On British conclusions about the Gulf War, see Louise Fawcett and Robert O'Neill, "Britain, the Gulf Crisis and European Security," in Gnesotto and Roper, eds., *Western Europe and the Gulf*, pp. 141-158.

[13] See William H. Taft IV, "Die Europäische Sicherheit und die Lehren aus dem Golfkrieg," *NATO-Brief* 39, no. 3 (1991):7-11.

[14] For American conclusions about the Gulf War, see Patrick J. Garrity, *Why the Gulf War Still Matters: Foreign Perspectives on the War and the Future of International Security*, Report No. 16 (Los Alamos, NM: Center for National Security Studies, July 1993); and Michael Brenner and Phil Williams, *Europe and the United States: Security Policy Toward Europe in the 1990s*, Internal Studies, no. 36 (Sankt Augustin: Konrad Adenauer Stiftung, 1992), p. 35.

[15] For Dumas-Genscher, see "Security Policy Cooperation Within the Framework of the Common Foreign and Security Policy of the Political Union," February 4, 1991, *Europe Documents*, February 21, 1991, p. 2. For Lamers-Fuchs, see Karl Lamers, "Eine Sicherheits-Union—Möglichkeiten und Grenzen: Zu einer deutsch-französischen Parlamentarier Initiative," in *Dokumente* 47 (February 1991):17-22.

[16] See Jacques Delors' March 7, 1991, Alastair Buchan Memorial Lecture at the International Institute for Strategic Studies, published as "European Integration and Security," *Survival* 23, no. 2 (March-April 1991):99-109.

[17] The description of the allied debates over security institutions draws from and updates my *French Security Policy After the Cold War*, pp. 20-25. For the most important Franco-German security initiatives leading up to Maastricht, see: "Text of Statement by Mitterrand and Kohl on EC Union," Reuter Press Agency, transcript, April 19, 1990; "Letter sent by German Chancellor Kohl and French President Mitterrand to the EC Chairman," FBIS-WEU-90-238, December 1, 1990, p. 1; "Security Policy Cooperation Within the Framework of the Common Foreign and Security Policy of the Political Union," February 4, 1991, *Europe Documents*, February 21, 1991, p. 2; and the text of the October 1991 Kohl-Mitterrand letter to the Dutch EC presidency calling for a European corps (discussed below) in *Le Monde*, October 17, 1991, p. 4.

[18] The British view was clearly expressed by Foreign Secretary Douglas Hurd: "An approach which emphasized the separateness of Europe would seriously weaken our real security. . . . The common foreign and security policy should include some broad security issues . . . but it should not compete with the military tasks in NATO." See Douglas Hurd, "No European defence identity without NATO," *Financial Times*, April 15, 1991, p. 13.

[19] For the Maastricht decisions on foreign and security policy, see the Treaty on European Union, article J. The decisions on the WEU's links with NATO were taken at a separate WEU meeting on December 10, 1991. See the "Declaration of the Member States of Western European Union which are also members of the European Union on the role of WEU and its relations with the European Union and with the Atlantic Alliance," December 10, 1991, text furnished by WEU Secretariat-General, published later as annex 5 of the Maastricht treaty.

[20] For the original proposals, see the text of the Mitterrand-Kohl proposal in "MM. Mitterrand et Kohl proposent de renforcer les responsabilités européennes en matière de défense," *Le Monde*, October 17, 1991, pp. 1, 4-5; or "Paris und Bonn wollen den Kern einer europäischen Armee schaffen," *Frankfurter Allgemeine Zeitung*, October 17, 1991, p. 1. The text can also be found reprinted in *Europa Archiv* 46, no. 22 (1991):D571-D574. The exact text called for expanding the joint brigade into "the basis for a European corps, to which the armed forces of other WEU member-states could be added."

[21] Just as the 1963 treaty came on the heels of a failed union initiative, the Franco-German corps proposal followed failed suggestions that the WEU create its own

multinational forces. These included not only the French and German proposals already mentioned but an April 1990 suggestion by WEU secretary-general Willem van Eekelen. See "WEU erwägt multinationale Brigaden," *Süddeutsche Zeitung*, April 24, 1990.

[22] Spanish defense minister Julian Garcia Vargas said, "From the outset, we have viewed sympathetically the Franco-German initiative, and we will take a positive decision on it in due course." See the interview with Mr. Vargas in *El Pais*, May 24, 1992, p. 16. On the Belgian decision, see Jacques Isnard, "L'armée Belge prévoit d'entrer dans l'Eurocorps," *Le Monde*, March 13, 1993; and Jean de la Guérvière, "La Belgique rejoindra bientôt l'Eurocorps," *Le Monde*, March 14, 1993. By the end of 1993, there was speculation that Spain would soon announce a formal contribution of a brigade (3,000-4,000 troops) to the Eurocorps. See Patrice Burchkalter, "Le Corps européen: Premier outil au service d'une politique européenne de défense," Agence France Presse, Informations générales, November 4, 1993.

[23] For van den Broek, see "L'Europe ne doit pas être soumise au consensus franco-allemand," *Le Monde*, October 18, 1991; and "Les Pays-Bas se disent 'outrés' par les méthodes de MM. Dumas et Genscher," *Le Monde*, October 9, 1991. For Rognoni, see Riccardo Orizio, "Roma non si arruola nell'Eurocorpo," *Corriere Della Sera*, May 27, 1992, p. 12. Rognoni later stated that the Maastricht treaty "did not ask us to act two by two, but all together in common." Rognoni is cited in William Drozdiak, "U.S.-French Tensions Called Peril to Alliance," *Washington Post*, May 27, 1992, p. A21. Also see "Bonn a défendu le projet de corps franco-allemand," *Le Monde*, May 28, 1992, p. 4.

[24] Interviews with SPD analysts and politicians in Bonn, fall 1992. Also see SPD deputy parliamentary group leader Norbert Gansel's concerns about parliamentary control, premature creation of armed forces for a political union, and "binationalization" in "Kohl antwortet im Bundestag auf Bedenken und Fragen der Nato-Partner," *Frankfurter Allgemeine Zeitung*, November 6, 1991.

[25] On the American reactions, see in particular Andrew Denison, "Amerika und das Eurokorps, *Europäische Sicherheit* (March 1993):123-126; Anne Engels, "Die USA und der Europäische Pfeiler 1984-92: WEU und deutsch-französische Sicherheitskooperation aus amerikanischer Sicht," unpublished master's thesis, Bonn University, 1993, pp. 68-75; and Karen E. Donfried, *The Franco-German Eurocorps: Implications for the U.S. Security Role in Europe* (Washington, DC: Congressional Research Service Report for Congress, October 22, 1992).

[26] For Cheney, see Alan Riding, "French and Germans Plan an Army Corps Despite NATO Fears," *New York Times*, May 23, 1992, p. 4. For Powell, see Denison, "Amerika und das Eurokorps," p. 123. For Galvin, see Donfried, *The Franco-German Eurocorps*, p. 15. For an example of qualified support for the Eurocorps by a number of high-level former U.S. officials, see *The Franco-German Corps and the Future of European Security: Implications for U.S. Policy* (Washington, D.C.: Foreign Policy Institute Policy Consensus Report, June 1992).

[27] For Taft, to undermine NATO structures through European arrangements would be "the height of folly." Cited in Engels, *Die USA und der Europäische Pfeiler*, p. 68. Also see Karl Feldmeyer, "Streit um das Europäische Korps," *Frankfurter Allgemeine Zeitung*, May 27, 1992, p. 5; and Marc Fisher, "Germans Caught in U.S.-French Rift," *Washington Post*, June 27, 1992, p. A15.

[28] Taft speech at the International Institute for Strategic Studies in February 1991, cited in Engels, *Die USA und der Europäische Pfeiler*, p. 41.

[29] See Bush cited in "After the Fall, an Identity Crisis," *The Boston Globe*, November 9, 1991, p. 14.

[30] See Dumas cited in Drozdiak, "U.S.-French Tensions Called Peril to Alliance," p. A21. Interviews conducted at the State Department during 1992-1993 confirm the relatively hostile nature of the American response.

[31] A good and detailed discussion of these aspects of the Eurocorps can be found in Scott A. Harris and James B. Steinberg, *European Defense and the Future of Transatlantic Relations*, MR-276 (Santa Monica, CA: RAND, 1993), pp. 12-33.

[32] Discussions have been taking place over a possible integration of the corps logistical support. Whereas one alternative foresees a forward base that would be divided into three national sectors for each nation participating in the corps, a second, more integrated version foresees a single and truly integrated forward logistical base. As of late 1993, French, German, and Belgian military officers were studying the problem to see if the latter alternative was feasible (interviews with French and German military officials in Bonn, August 1993).

[33] See "Summit of the Franco-German Defense and Security Council on May 22, 1991 in La Rochelle," press release provided by Embassy of the Federal Republic of Germany, Washington DC, May 26, 1992.

[34] See William Drozdiak, "France, Germany Unveil Corps as a Step Toward European Defense," *Washington Post*, May 23, 1992, p. A15.

[35] See, for example, the German agreement at La Rochelle that the Eurocorps forces would be given "as a priority" to the corps, and Foreign Minister Kinkel's assurance to U.S. Secretary of State James Baker in Lisbon one week later that NATO had first rights ("Das erste Zugriffsrecht hat die NATO"). For the La Rochelle commitment, see Henri de Bresson and Claire Tréan, "Paris et Bonn protestent de leur fidélité à l'OTAN," *Le Monde*, May 22, 1992, pp. 1, 6; For Kinkel, see Klaus-Dieter Frankenberger, "Tragende Säulen geraten ins Wanken," *Frankfurter Allgemeine Zeitung*, May 29, 1992. As discussed below, this was only one of many instances of Germany trying to find middle ground between the French and American positions.

[36] See David Buchan, "Paris Agrees on Nato Role in Eurocorps," *Financial Times*, December 1, 1992, p. 2; Joseph Fitchett, "Paris Concedes to NATO on French-German Corps," *International Herald Tribune*, December 1, 1992, p. 1; and "Abkommen über das Euro-Korps gebilligt," *Frankfurter Allgemeine Zeitung*, December 24, 1992.

[37] See Karl Feldmeyer, "Einbindung des deutsch-französischen Korps in das

atlantische Bündnis," *Frankfurter Allgemeine Zeitung*, December 5, 1992; and David Buchan, "Paris Agrees on Nato Role in Eurocorps," *Financial Times*, December 1, 1992, p. 2.

[38] Just after the La Rochelle summit, for example, Mitterrand said: "We don't want to see American troops leave, but who knows what decisions will be made because of economic difficulties facing the American leadership?" See Mitterrand cited in Drozdiak, "France, Germany Unveil Corps as Step Toward European Defense," p. A15. Former prime minister Michel Rocard has made the French case this way: "Can Europeans be confronted with crises that do not concern the United States? To some, the very idea was seen as a blow to transatlantic solidarity. The conflict in Yugoslavia has changed all that. Rightly or wrongly, the United States decided that its interest and ideas of international stability were not at stake in this crisis, and it let the EC act independently. This is the type of crisis Europe is likely to face in the years to come, and it illustrates why Europe must have the military means to support its policies." See Rocard's November 1991 Leffingwell Lecture to the Council on Foreign Relations in New York, published as *Europe and the United States*, Critical Issues no. 2 (New York: Council on Foreign Relations Press, 1992), p. 14. The Americans, of course, complained that this could become a self-fulfilling prophecy: the more the French did to compensate for a supposed American departure, the more they would provoke just that.

[39] Interview with German diplomat at German embassy in Washington DC, May 1992. Other German diplomats suggested the Eurocorps was primarily an effort by Chancellor Kohl to maintain good relations with Mitterrand and the French, who were reportedly disappointed with Germany's agreement to join NATO's Rapid Reaction Corps in May 1991 (interviews in Bonn, winter 1991-1992).

[40] Senior French official cited in Drozdiak, "U.S.-French Tensions Called Peril to Alliance," p. A21. On the different French and German perspectives, see the telling comment by a German official: "I don't know whom to believe anymore . . . The moment I report to my French colleagues what the Americans said Paris told them, they get terribly excited and deny saying any such thing" (Bonn official who speaks daily to senior diplomats in Washington and Paris, cited in Fisher, "Germans Caught in U.S.-French Rift," p. A 15).

[41] Interviews in Bonn and Paris, winter and spring 1993. Also see the comment by a "senior official in Bonn" that the agreement would "quietly open the door for all French forces" (cited in Fitchett, "Paris Concedes to NATO on French-German Corps," *International Herald Tribune*, December 1, 1992, pp. 1, 6).

[42] For the announcement that "logic required French forces in Germany to return home," see "La logique voudra que l'armée française regagne son pays," *Le Monde*, July 8-9, 1990.

[43] German acceptance of peacekeeping/peacemaking missions through the corps was made contingent upon "the resolution of German constitutional questions." See "Summit of the Franco-German Defense and Security Council on May 22, 1991 in La Rochelle," press release provided by Embassy of the Federal Republic

of Germany, Washington, DC, May 26, 1992.

[44] See David S. Yost, "France and West European Defence Identity," *Survival* 33, no. 4 (1991):327-351.

[45] In this section, "Eastern Europe" and "the East" will refer to the entire European area of former Soviet domination. "Central Europe" will refer specifically to Poland, the former Czechoslovakia, and Hungary.

[46] For figures on Poland and Russia, see Robert Gerald Livingston, "United Germany: Bigger and Better," *Foreign Policy* 87 (summer 1992):167. For Germans in Ukraine, see the report in the *Süddeutsche Zeitung*, March 2, 1992.

[47] See the chart under the title "Facing a Troubled Future?" published in the *International Herald Tribune*, June 29, 1993, p. 6.

[48] See Tom Redburn, "Germany Fuels East's Industrial Rebirth," *International Herald Tribune*, March 5, 1993. In terms of direct investments in Central Europe, Italian and American firms—not French—followed German firms on the list of leaders by country. See "Privatisierung bietet Anreiz für ausländische Investoren," *Handelsblatt*, October 16, 1992; and the chart on German investment in Eastern Europe provided in the *Washington Post*, April 17, 1994, p. A25.

[49] On aid to the former Soviet Union, see "German Support for the Transition to Democracy and Market Economy in the Former Soviet Union," (New York: German Information Service, June 1992). On aid to Central and Eastern Europe, see Organization of Economic Cooperation and Development, *Development Co-operation* (Paris: OECD, 1994), pp. 128-151. On Germany's role in Eastern Europe more generally, see Anne-Marie Le Gloannec, "The Implications of German Unification for Western Europe," in Paul B. Stares, ed., *The New Germany and the New Europe* (Washington DC: The Brookings Institution, 1992), p. 271.

[50] Of the 16 million people currently studying German in primary, secondary, and post-secondary institutions worldwide, 12 million are in East-Central Europe and the Soviet Union. See Andrei S. Markovits and Simon Reich, *The New Face of Germany: Gramsci, Neorealism and Hegemony*, Center for European Studies Working Paper Series no. 28 (Cambridge: Harvard University Press, n.d.), who cite German foreign ministry documents from 1990 as their sources. Moreover, with Germany the leading trading partner for all of the countries of Central and Eastern Europe (accounting for an expected 30-35 percent of total trade by 1995, and more than 50 percent for Poland, the former Czechoslovakia, and Hungary), the incentive for the East Europeans to focus on Germany and German is bound to grow further. See Andras Inotai, "Economic Implications of German Unification for Central and Eastern Europe," in Stares, ed., *The New Germany*, p. 294-295.

[51] For the original confederation proposal, see Claire Tréan, "M. Mitterrand souhaite une 'confédération' européenne avec les pays de l'Est," *Le Monde*, January 2, 1990, pp. 1, 5.

[52] See Mitterrand cited in *Le Monde*, June 14, 1991. Previously, Mitterrand had often made the case that "it would be wise to improve the cohesion of the Twelve before going further" (cited in *Le Monde*, June 20, 1990, p. 1).

[53] Interviews, May 1992. As late as 1992, Mitterrand was still arguing, "We need a permanent structure in which the member states of the EC can build the future Europe in equality with the other states of Europe." See "Mitterrand für europäische Konföderation," *Frankfurter Allgemeine Zeitung*, March 2, 1992. On Central European objections, also see the discussion of Stanley Hoffmann, who served as a rapporteur at the Prague meeting, in his "French Dilemmas ar ' Strategies in the New Europe," in Robert O. Keohane, Joseph S. Nye and Stanley Hoffmann, *After the Cold War: International Institutions and State Strategies in Europe, 1989-1991* (Cambridge: Harvard University Press, 1993), p. 141.

[54] Cited in Livingston, "United Germany," p. 166.

[55] On French objections to the NACC, see Gordon, *French Security Policy after the Cold War*, p. 17.

[56] On France's grudging acceptance of the NACC, see Jean de la Guérvière, "La France acceuille avec scepticisme le projet de 'Conseil de coopération de l'Atlantique nord,'" *Le Monde*, October 30, 1991. On the gradual opening to the notion of widening the EC, see Le Gloannec, "The Implications of German Unification," p. 272. On France's increasing imports from Eastern Europe, see James B. Steinberg, *"An Ever Closer Union": European Integration and its Implications for the Future of U.S.-European Relations*, R-4177-A (Santa Monica, CA: RAND, 1993), p. 116.

[57] See, for example, the arguments of Edouard Balladur, "Le monde change, il faut changer la politique aussi: La France et le nouvel ordre planétaire," *Le Figaro*, February 2, 1992, pp. 1, 6; and those of Pierre Lellouche in "Pour une nouvelle donne franco-allemande," *Le Monde*, February 24, 1993; and "La France, l'OTAN et le Nouveau Monde," four-part series in *Le Figaro*, July 18-26, 1992.

[58] For RPR calls to "widen" the EC, see Alain Juppé, "Oui, si . . . à Maastricht," *Le Monde*, April 21, 1991; Edouard Balladur, "Le monde change," pp. 1, 6; and Daniel Carton, "Le RPR et l'UDF continuent de s'opposer sur l'avenir de l'Europe," *Le Monde*, April 16, 1992. For Balladur on NATO, see "Le monde change," p. 6.

[59] See Nicholas Milletitch, "Paris et Prague pourraient organiser des formations militaires communes," Agence France Presse, Informations générales, August 26, 1993.

[60] See "M. Balladur a présenté son 'pacte pour la stabilité et la sécurité en Europe'," *Le Monde*, June 11, 1993; and the "Summary Report" provided by the French embassy, Washington, DC, author's text.

[61] Interviews in Bonn, May 1993.

[62] See Christine Courcol, "Les nouvelles démocraties d'Europe centrale s'impatientent," Agence France Presse, Informations générales, September 2, 1993; David B. Ottaway, "Slovakia Joins Neighbors in Call for NATO Entry," *Washington Post*, January 5, 1994, p. A21; and the interview with Polish president Lech Walesa discussed in John Pomfret, "Walesa Warns Communism May Reemerge," *Washington Post*, January 4, 1994, pp. A1, A12.

[63] See Rühe's March 26, 1993, Alastair Buchan Memorial Lecture at the Inter-

national Institute for Strategic Studies in London, published as "Shaping Euro-Atlantic Policies: A Grand Strategy for a New Era," in *Survival* 35, no. 2 (summer 1993):129-137.

[64] See Judy Dempsey, "Kinkel Urges Stronger Ties With the East," *Financial Times*, December 31, 1993, p. 2; and Quentin Peel and Lionel Barber, "Germany Wants Eastern Europe in Nato and EC," *Financial Times*, September 11, 1993, p. 24. As of May 1993, Kinkel was calling only for NATO to "reflect on finding a 'middle way' between full NATO membership and exclusion from the alliance. For Kinkel, see "Auf der Suche nach einem Mittelweg," *Frankfurter Allgemeine Zeitung*, March 6, 1993, p. 5. For Lamers, interviews with Lamers's advisers, July 1993.

[65] Interviews at NATO, June 1993. Also see Judy Dempsey, "Germany's Ministries in Nato Accord," *Financial Times*, January 7, 1994.

[66] See Yacine Le Forestier, "M. Léotard: Paris veut 'travailler davantage' avec l'OTAN sur ses missions nouvelles," Agence France Presse, Informations générales, August 25, 1993.

[67] Interviews with French officials, June 1993.

[68] On the American debate, see George Graham, "Quest for a Strategy: A Look at the Debates in Nato over its Future Shape," *Financial Times*, August 31, 1993.

[69] See David White, "Nato's Unequal Partnership for Peace," *Financial Times*, January 11, 1994, p. 3. On the Poland proposal, see David B. Ottaway, "War Games in Poland Proposed," *Washington Post*, January 8, 1994, pp. A1, A18.

[70] See Quentin Peel, "Bonn and Paris Plan EU Ostpolitik," *Financial Times*, March 25, 1994.

[71] See Quentin Peel, "Kohl Says Door Must be Open to Central Europe," *Financial Times*, March 24, 1994.

[72] See Ministère de la Défense, *Livre Blanc sur la Défense, 1994* (Paris: Service d'Information et de Relations Publiques des Armées, Ministère de la Défense, 1994), p. 38. The White Paper adds (on the same page) that "the extension of alliances would not suffice in solving the problems, such as those involving borders or minorities, that have emerged with virulence and constitute potential areas of serious crises."

[73] On the dispute over Germany's role in the negotiations, see Quentin Peel and David Buchan, "Enlargement of EU Strains Franco-German Axis: Anxiety in Paris over the Future of the Union Has Led to Criticism of 'Heavy Handed' Tactics by Bonn," *Financial Times*, March 17, 1994, p. 20. Also see David Buchan and Quentin Peel, "Odd Couple's Testing Tiffs: David Buchan and Quentin Peel Examine Emerging Strains in a Relationship That Has Underpinned European Unity for Decades," *Financial Times*, March 18, 1994, p. 19.

[74] The absolute figures give an even better sense of the difference: In 1992, France took $55.8 million worth of German exports and provided $48.8 million of German imports. The respective figures for Poland were $4.6 million and $4.8 million. See International Monetary Fund, *Direction of Trade Statistics Year-*

book (Washington, DC: International Monetary Fund, 1993), pp. 177, 184.

[75] The evolution of Genscher's position in the summer of 1991 is discussed in Harald Müller, "German Foreign Policy After Unification," in Stares, ed., *The New Germany*, p. 150.

[76] On the WEU rejection of the buffer force idea, see "Le rejet, par les Douze, d'une intervention militaire immédiate constitue un échec pour la France et l'Allemagne," *Le Monde*, September 21, 1991, p. 3.

[77] For Kohl's promise to Croatia and Slovenia, see *Bulletin*, Presse und Informationsamt der Bundesregierung, No. 140 (Bonn: December 10, 1991), p. 1144.

[78] The conditions to be met by the Yugoslav republics included: (1)respect for the dispositions of the United Nations on law, democracy, and human rights; (2)guarantees on rights for ethnic and national groups as well as minorities; (3)respect of the inviolability of all borders, which can only be modified by peaceful means and mutual agreement; and (4)acceptance of the engagements undertaken by Yugoslavia on disarmament, nuclear proliferation, and regional security and stability. See "L'indépendance des républiques yougoslaves," *Le Monde*, December 18, 1991; and the text of the Badinter Plan in *Bulletin*, Presse und Informationsamt der Bundesregierung, No. 144/S1173 (Bonn: December 19, 1991), pp. 1173-74. On the recognition episode in general, also see Catherine Guicherd, *L'heure de l'Europe: premières leçons du conflit yougoslave* (Paris: Les Cahiers du Crest, March 1993), no. 10, pp. 16-17; and John Newhouse, "The Diplomatic Round: Dodging the Problem," *The New Yorker*, August 24, 1992, pp. 60-71.

[79] One observer has written that at the December 16-17 meetings, Germany had Italian, Belgian, and Danish support in favor of recognition, while France, Spain, Greece, and the Netherlands "remained most resolute in favor of preserving Yugoslavia's unity," and the United Kingdom was "somewhere in the middle." See James B. Steinberg, *The Role of European Institutions in Security After the Cold War: Some Lessons from Yugoslavia*, N-3445-FF (Santa Monica, CA: RAND, 1992), p. 15. For German arguments that recognition was not a unilateral German move (what some Germans now call the "Anerkennungslüge" [recognition lie]), see Joseph Fitchett, "Bonn Claims Recognition Will Help End Yugoslav War," *International Herald Tribune*, January 16, 1992, pp. 1-2; Marc Fisher, "Bonn Angrily Rebuffs U.S. Charge It Provoked Yugoslav Crisis, *International Herald Tribune*, June 19-20, 1993, p. 1; Immo Stabreit (German ambassador to the United States), "The Charge Is Serbia's to Answer," *International Herald Tribune*, July 1, 1993, p. 4 (Stabreit calls recognition a "unanimous decision by the 12 member states of the European Community"); and interviews in Bonn by author, 1992-1993. French disagreement with the recognition policy was suggested by Foreign Minister Roland Dumas's question, "Where is the spirit of Maastricht?" and a Dutch official's comment that "in this case, at least, the Germans don't give a damn about European unity," which suggest an outstanding disagreement among Europeans even after December 17. Officials cited in William Drozdiak, "Germany Vows Balkan Recognition,"

Washington Post, January 11, 1992, p. A14. Also see "La France reste réservée à l'idée de reconnaître la Croatie," *Le Monde*, January 12-13, 1992.

[80] See, for example, Newhouse, "The Diplomatic Round," p. 65; and George Soros, "Prospect for European Disintegration," speech delivered to the Aspen Institute Berlin on September 29, 1993 (New York: George Soros Foundation, September 1993), p. 6.

[81] For an excellent analysis of German motivations, see Heinz-Jürgen Axt, "Hat Genscher Jugoslawien entzweit? Mythen und Fakten zur Aussenpolitik des vereinten Deutschlands," *Europa Archiv* 12 (1993):351-360. Other good sources include Werner A. Perger, "Warum Bonn am Pranger steht," *Die Zeit* 26 (June 25, 1993):5; Beverly Crawford, "German Foreign Policy After the Cold War: The Decision to Recognize Croatia," University of California Center for German and European Studies Working Paper 2.21, August 1993; and Müller, "German Foreign Policy after Unification," pp. 150-154.

[82] Catholic bishops in Germany spoke out from the very beginning of the Yugoslavia war for support of their fellow believers in Slovenia and Croatia. See Quentin Peel, "Germans Instinctively Back Self-determination," *Financial Times*, December 16, 1991, p. 2. Also see the repeated comments of *Frankfurter Allgemeine Zeitung* editor Johann-Georg Reißmuller to the effect that "the Croats are among the columns of the Catholic global church." This citation is from the *Frankfurter Allgemeine Zeitung*, November 16, 1991, p. 1.

[83] The influence of the Yugoslav minority should not be exaggerated in explaining German support for Croatian independence; unlike American ethnic groups that often vote, organize, raise money, and lobby, the Yugoslav minorities in Germany are politically relatively silent. See Alexander Mühlen, "Die deutsche Rolle bei der Anerkennung der jugoslawischen Sezessionsstaaten," *Liberal* 2 (June 1992):53. For two suggestions that the Yugoslav minority did matter, see Hanns W. Maull, "Germany's New Foreign Policy," in Hanns W. Maull and Philip H. Gordon, *German Foreign Policy and the German "National Interest": German and American Perspectives*, Seminar Papers, no. 5 (Washington, DC: American Institute for Contemporary German Studies, January 1993), p. 12; and Hans Stark, "Dissonances franco-allemandes sur fond de guerre serbo-croate," *Politique étrangère* (February 1992):341. Maull writes of the Croat community in Germany as having "good political contacts" in all the major parties and the backing of the Catholic Church, and Stark writes of "formidable pressures exercised by the pro-independence lobby of nearly 700,000 immigrant workers."

[84] Regarding the SPD leaders, several of whom made a hasty visit to Slovenia and Croatia in late summer 1991, see "Gansel-Bericht fordert Anerkennung Sloweniens und Kroatiens; Föderation souveräner Staaten vorgeschlagen," *Archiv der Gegenwart* 14 (June 28-July 7, 1991):35795-35797; the report on a trip by SPD officials to Yugoslavia in June 1991 in the *Frankfurter Allgemeine Zeitung*, June 27, 1991; and the discussion in "Ein großer Erfolg für uns," *Der Spiegel*, December 23, 1991, p. 19. SPD foreign policy spokesman Norbert Gansel com-

mented that "if the EC sticks to its plans (for delayed recognition), it will end up recognizing no more than corpses and ruins" (cited in "Ein großer Erfolg für uns," p. 19.

[85] See, for example, the arguments of Hans-Dietrich Genscher in "Für Recht auf Selbstbestimmung," *Das Parlament*, November 15/22, 1991, p. 7.

[86] Rühe concluded with the remark, "We should start a movement in the EC to lead to such recognition" (cited in *Guardian*, July 2, 1991, p. 8).

[87] For a comparison of the German and French concepts of nationhood, see Rogers Brubacker, *Citizenship and Nationhood in France and Germany* (Cambridge: Harvard University Press, 1992).

[88] On the German tendency to see problems in a legalistic fashion, see the analysis of Wolfram F. Hanrieder, *Germany, America, Europe: Forty Years of German Foreign Policy* (New Haven: Yale University Press, 1989), especially chap. 6.

[89] See the interview with Genscher under the title "Die Welt ist von Grund auf verändert," *Die Zeit* 36 (August 30, 1991):6.

[90] One observer attributes Germany's hope that recognition would help stop the war to a certain German idealism missing in Britain and France. In German minds, "people killing each other as in 1941 . . . was not supposed to happen—ever again. The Allies wouldn't permit it." See Newhouse, "The Diplomatic Round," p. 64.

[91] The notion that German "hubris" and sense of "knowing better" was cited by a number of German colleagues and interview sources as the best explanation for German behavior toward Yugoslavia in the winter of 1991-1992.

[92] Mitterrand cited in "Mitterrand erwartet neue Formen der Zusammenarbeit," *Frankfurter Allgemeine Zeitung*, September 13, 1991. Also see the concerns expressed by Mitterrand at a February 29, 1992, conference in Paris on "the Tribes of Europe," discussed in André Fontaine, "L'Europe et ses frontières," *Le Monde*, March 10, 1992.

[93] See Stephen M. Walt, "Alliances: Balancing and Bandwagoning," in Robert J. Art and Robert Jervis, eds., *International Politics: Enduring Concepts and Contemporary Issues*, 3rd ed. (New York: Harper Collins Publishers, 1992) p. 70-78.

[94] For an expression of the French view that Slovenia and Croatia would be German-oriented, see Luc Rosenzweig, "L'Allemagne, puissance protectrice des Slovenes et des Croates," *Le Monde*, July 4, 1991, p. 4.

[95] See Rudolph Chimelli, "Bosnien helfen, Serbien nicht verprellen," *Süddeutsche Zeitung*, August 22-23, 1992, p. 8. For other examples, see the French government's statement at the time of a May 1991 visit of Yugoslav prime minister Ante Markovic about "the tradition of friendly [Franco-Serbian/Yugoslav relations]" and "the fraternity of arms of the First and Second World Wars"; and Roland Dumas's response later in the year to a question about France as Serbia's "protector" that "France and Serbia have had preferential ties in the past." For the first statement, see the French foreign ministry's *Bulletin d'information du ministère des Affaires étrangères*, May 24, 1991; for the second, see Dumas cited in *Libération*, December 6, 1991, p. 18, cited in Steinberg, *European Institutions*, p. 43.

[96] See, for example, the article by Jean-Yves Heller, "Etre Serbe en Croatie," *Le Monde*, October 21, 1991, pp. 1, 5.

[97] See Alain Juppé's criticism of France's unwillingness during 1992 to name Serbia the aggressor and impose sanctions on it, in "Un entretien avec Alain Juppé," *Le Monde*, September 2, 1993.

[98] Author's interview with a senior State Department official, Washington, DC, May 1992.

[99] British foreign secretary Hurd often referred (at least implicitly) to painful lessons learned by Britain from its intervention in Northern Ireland when warning about getting involved in ethnic conflicts. See William Drozdiak, "EC Balks at Sending Force to Yugoslavia," *Washington Post*, September 20, 1991, p. A19.

[100] See Hurd in *London Times*, December 3, 1991, p. 14. American sources often warned against recognition, using the same arguments; see, for example, the *Washington Post* editorial "Recognizing Croatia and Slovenia," *Washington Post*, December 24, 1991.

[101] The Bosnian declaration of independence resulted from a referendum held on February 29 and March 1, 1992, that was massively positive but was boycotted by most of Bosnia's Serb population (which had already begun to set up its own "republic"). The Bosnian government had opposed recognition but accepted holding the referendum that was suggested by the Badinter Commission on Yugoslavia. See "Conférence pour la paix en Yougoslavie," Commission d'Arbitrage, avis no. 4, January 11, 1992; and the discussion in Guicherd, *l'Heure de l'Europe*, p. 18.

[102] Mitterrand explained, "The attitude that I defended in Luxembourg in June 1991, when we were first called upon to deal with this affair, was to delay the recognition of the former Yugoslav republics until the international community had guaranteed the rights of minorities. In my view the major error was committed a few months later under the pressure of events. To recognize the independence and sovereignty of new states without having obtained the guarantees that I requested was to expose oneself to the tragedies that followed." See "M. Mitterrand affirme qu'il résiste à la poussée générale pour l'emploi de la force," *Le Monde*, January 22, 1993.

[103] For Dumas, see "Roland Dumas met en cause les responsabilités 'écrasantes' de l'Allemagne et du Vatican dans 'l'accélération de la crise," *Le Monde*, June 22, 1993, p. 3. Also see former prime minister Fabius's argument that recognition accelerated the war in "Un entretien avec Laurent Fabius," *Le Monde*, February 20, 1993.

[104] For Christopher, see the interview in *USA Today*, June 18, 1993. For Vance, see David Binder, "Vance, Leaving, Sees Hope for Bosnia Plan Despite Fighting," *New York Times*, April 14, 1993, p. A8.

[105] Foreign Minister Kinkel stated that Christopher's version of events was "factually not correct," and German ambassador to Washington Immo Stabreit, who was sent to the State Department to "make clear the facts of the case," responded in a column published in major English-language newspapers that allegations that

Germany provoked the tragedy in Bosnia was "the creation of a legend." See Stabreit, "The Charge is Serbia's to Answer," p. 4; and Fisher, "Bonn Angrily Rebuffs U.S. Charge It Provoked Yugoslav Crisis," pp. 1, 5. Also see "Kinkel verteidigt Anerkennungspolitik," *Süddeutsche Zeitung*, June 18, 1993, p. 1; "Trübungen zwischen Bonn und Washington," *Frankfurter Allgemeine Zeitung*, June 19, 1993, p. 1; and the editorial, "Christophers Sündenbock" (Christopher's scapegoat), in the same edition.

[106] The sanctions to which France agreed included a ban on trade, a freeze of foreign assets, and a ban on air traffic to and from Serbia. France, however, continued to oppose a UN move to take away "successor-state" status from Serbia/ Montenegro for the former Yugoslavia. See Newhouse, "The Diplomatic Round," p. 68.

[107] On American and European criticism, see David Binder, "U.S. Is Worried by Bonn's New Assertiveness," *International Herald Tribune*, January 7, 1992, pp. 1-2; Marc Fisher, "Germany Facing Harsher Criticism," *Washington Post*, March 31, 1992, p. A11; and "Kohl weist antideutsche Äußerungen Özals zurück," *Frankfurter Allgemeine Zeitungen*, March 31, 1992, p. 1.

[108] For Kinkel, see "Die Verteidiger von Srebrenica kapitulieren: UN-Friedenstruppen rücken in die Stadt ein," *Frankfurter Allgemeine Zeitung*, April 19, 1993, pp. 1-2. For Rühe, see "Gleiche Verantwortung übernehmen wie alle anderen" (interview with Rühe), *Süddeutsche Zeitung*, February 13-14, 1993, p. 12.

[109] On the no-fly zone, see Claire Tréan, "La France 'prendra sa part' dans une action contre l'aviation serbe en Bosnie," *Le Monde*, December 29, 1992, p. 1. On the airdrops, see "France Joins Airdrop Effort over Muslim Town in Bosnia," *International Herald Tribune*, March 25, 1993. On the five-country "Washington Plan," see "U.S. and Four Nations Join Plan to Curb Fighting in Bosnia," *New York Times*, May 23, 1993, p. 1.

[110] See, for example, President Mitterrand's July 1993 comment that "France has been, among all countries, the one that has been most present [in Yugoslavia] since the beginning, that has proposed everything: legal methods, international arbitration, the presence of troops to serve as a buffer, to fulfill a humanitarian duty. We have more than 5,000 men there. The country that has the most after us has no more than 2,500, and how many [countries] haven't sent any at all? I am not incriminating them, but look, there are not Germans, their constitution opposes it, there are no Americans, there are not Italians." See "Interview télévisé du Président de la République," *Le Monde*, July 16, 1993. Foreign Minister Juppé also often underscores France's exceptional role in Yugoslavia. See "Un entretien avec "Alain Juppé: 'Il faut s'accrocher bec et ongles à la construction européenne," *Le Monde*, September 2, 1993.

[111] See, on this point, the statements made by Chancellor Kohl at the 1993 Munich Conference on Security Policy; Foreign Minister Kinkel's June 1992 statement that "because of German history, the Bundeswehr should not participate [in

Yugoslavia], and FDP party leader Otto Graf Lambsdorff's indicative comment that "we were [in Yugoslavia] fifty years ago, that's enough." For Kohl, see Josef Joffe, "Übrig bleibt die Allianz," *Süddeutsche Zeitung*, February 8, 1993, p. 4. For Kinkel, see "Kinkel Appeals to Serbian Leadership to 'Stop Murder and Destruction,'" in *This Week in Germany* (New York: German Information Center, June 12, 1992), p. 1. Lambsdorff cited in "FDP gegen deutschen Militäreinsatz in Bosnien," *Süddeutsche Zeitung*, January 19, 1993.

[112] See the arguments used by the SPD opposition during the Bundestag debate in *Deut..cher Bundestag: Stenographischer Bericht*, 101st sitting, Bonn, July 22, 1992, *Plenarprotokoll* (transcripts) 12, no. 101, 8636. On the spiked guns, see Josel Toffe, "The New Europe: Yesterday's Ghosts," *Foreign Affairs* 72, no. 1 (America and the World 1992/93):33.

[113] For the FDP's position that German pilots could not participate without a constitutional change, see "Keine militärische Aktivität ohne Grundgesetz-Änderung," *Frankfurter Allgemeine Zeitung*, January 26, 1993, p. 1. For SPD opposition and the lecision of the Constitutional Court, see "AWACS-Einsatz: Regierung bestätigt, Koalitionsfrieden auch," *Süddeutsche Zeitung*, April 13, 1993, p. 1.

[114] See "U.S. and Four Nations Join Plan to Curb Fighting in Bosnia," p. 1; and "Le 'programme d'action' de Washington continue de susciter de vives controverses entre alliés," *Le Monde*, May 28, 1993, p. 3.

[115] See Le Gloannec, "The Implications of German Unification," p. 259.

[116] Chancellor Kohl suggested reconsidering the arms embargo as early as January 1993 and reportedly pushed the idea on his European colleagues at a June meeting of the European Council in Copenhagen. Interviews conducted with German officials in Bonn during 1992-1993 suggest German support for lifting the arms embargo was widespread but muted largely in deference to the British and French. Regarding Kohl's suggestion, see "Kohl will Waffenembargo gegen Bosnien überdenken," *Süddeutsche Zeitung*, January 18, 1993. For the Copenhagen summit, see Alan Cowell, "Clinton Seems Committed to Lifting Bosnia Embargo," *International Herald Tribune*, June 26-27, 1993, pp. 1-2.

[117] See Eugene Robinson, "Britain Reaffirms Opposition to Lifting Bosnia Arms Ban," *International Herald Tribune*, April 20, 1993; and Roger Cohen, "France Joins the Fray Against U.S. on Arms for Bosnia," *International Herald Tribune*, April 22, 1993, p. 2.

[118] See Daniel Williams, "U.S., in Reversal, Yields to Europe on Bosnian Crisis," *International Herald Tribune*, May 18, 1993, p. 1. American officials have explained that Christopher was not sent to "convince" the Europeans but simply to listen to their views on what should be done. Whatever the case, the secretary of state found no support for American ideas.

[119] Britain, France, and Russia abstained from the vote on the American proposal, ensuring that it would not have the requisite eight votes in favor that it would have needed to pass. See Richard Bernstein, "U.S. Loses Bosnia Arms Vote,"

International Herald Tribune, July 1, 1993, p. 2.

[120] See, for example, the accusations by U.S. senator Joseph Biden that Europeans showed "hypocrisy and self-delusion" for opposing U.S. calls for air strikes, in "EC and U.S. Tempers Flare Over Dealing with War in Bosnia," *International Herald Tribune*, May 12, 1993, p. 1; the suggestion by Senators Richard Lugar and Bob Dole in a joint letter to President Clinton that the continuation of the war was due to "the pursuit of half-measures on the part of the Europeans and the United Nations," cited in Paul F. Horvitz, "Allies Defend Bosnia Plan, Hinting at Tougher Steps," *International Herald Tribune*, May 25, 1993; and President Clinton's own complaints that the British and French found it "far more important to avoid lifting the arms embargo than to save [Bosnia]," in Eugene Robinson, "Clinton's Remarks Cause Upper Lips to Twitch," *Washington Post*, October 19, 1993. The Europeans, in particular the French, responded that the Americans would be more helpful if they were to contribute forces on the ground rather than simply criticizing the Europeans (interviews in Paris and Bonn, spring 1993).

[121] See R.W. Apple, "The NATO Summit: NATO Again Plans Possible Air Raid on Serbs in Bosnia," *New York Times*, January 12, 1994, p. A1.

[122] See Elaine Sciolino with Douglas Jehl, "As U.S. Sought a Bosnia Policy, the French Offered a Good Idea," *New York Times*, February 14, 1994, pp. A1, A6. For the text of the NATO communiqué, see "NATO Communiqué Rejects Extension of Deadline," *Financial Times*, February 11, 1994, p. 2.

[123] For a few examples of the new hope following the success in Sarajevo, see Douglas Jehl, "Conflict in the Balkans: Clinton Now Hopes Calm in Sarajevo Can Be Broadened," *New York Times*, February 22, 1994, p. A1; Daniel Williams and Thomas W. Lippman, "Muslims and Croats to Link Territories: Step Aimed at Ending War in Bosnia," *Washington Post*, March 2, 1994; David B. Ottaway, "For Sarajevo, A Celebration of Normal Life," *Washington Post*, March 21, 1994; and Misha Glenny, "Hope for Bosnia?" *New York Review of Books*, April 7, 1994, pp. 6-8.

[124] A careful study of the dynamic setoff when the Communist bloc broke apart and national pressures emerged in this nationalist part of Europe might suggest that ethnic disintegration in Yugoslavia was inevitable and would have taken place regardless of the policies of outside powers. For a good sense of the seemingly inexorable march toward war and the crimes and mistakes committed on all sides, see Misha Glenny, *The Fall of Yugoslavia: The Third Balkan War* (New York: Penguin Books, 1992).

3

Post-Cold War Trends in French and German Security Policies

The end of the Cold War and German unification have radically changed the geopolitical environment in which French and German security policies are made. Although it would be wrong to conclude that these changes will fully transform the way France and Germany pursue cooperation with each other and with their allies, it would also be naive to believe that countries can experience changes of this magnitude without changing their policies significantly as well. It may be too soon to identify the national security policy patterns that will develop in France and Germany in the post-Cold War world—national orientations and institutional relationships are not changed overnight—but certain trends are already apparent. This chapter identifies conceptual and security policy trends in France and Germany and discusses their implications for the European and Atlantic alliances.

France
A More Cooperative Attitude Toward the United States and NATO

When the Cold War ended in 1989 and German unification took place in 1990, it was at least plausible that France would abandon its traditional reticence toward cooperation with NATO and the United States and adopt a more Atlanticist approach. Faced with a unified and more independent Germany as well as a Russia with an uncertain future, French leaders might have argued that a rapprochement with the United States was in France's strategic interest, an argument that would have gained ground with the lessons of the Gulf War about national military independence. The end of the Cold War would have been a convenient time for France to claim that its main geopolitical goal had been achieved and that its interests now required not liberating Europe from American influence but persuading the Americans to remain involved.[1]

Whatever the options at the time, an Atlantic rapprochement did not take place. Under the Socialists and Mitterrand from 1989 to early 1993, France refused to modify significantly its relationship with NATO, it resisted almost all of NATO's new initiatives, and it seemed to see NATO reform as designed to stifle the creation of a European security identity. By the end of 1992 France did agree to allow NATO to undertake some new functional and geographical tasks (specifically, peacekeeping on behalf of the UN or CSCE), and certain French leaders such as Defense Minister Pierre Joxe began calling for France "to participate more in the future than it has in the past in politico-military discussions."[2] But Mitterrand and Dumas remained opposed to any more fundamental change. Instead of seeking to reintegrate with NATO and giving the alliance a new role, Mitterrand reminded his allies that NATO was not a "holy alliance," and Dumas repeatedly made clear that "France's relations with NATO have not changed."[3]

The center-right opposition, rhetorically at least, adopted a different approach. Throughout the election campaign, nearly all leading members of the RPR—Union for French Democracy (UDF) coalition called on France to end what Alain Juppé called its "grumbling and conservative attitude" and instead to "reintegrate certain NATO organisms."[4] RPR leader Jacques Chirac and party security expert Pierre Lellouche repeatedly argued that "integration with 50,000 or 70,000 Americans in Europe will not have the same meaning as when the American contingent was 325,000" and attacked the "incomprehensible attitude of obstruction" within NATO.[5] Chirac adviser François Bujon de l'Estang argued that "the reasons that led France to take a singular position within NATO are no longer valid," and RPR defense expert Jacques Baumel maintained that "the time has come to get away from ambiguities" and to be present where forces and missions are decided—NATO.[6] Chirac's candid statement to a group of French reserve officers in February 1993 sums up the extent of the new tone in French thinking about NATO and the United States:

> With respect to Europe, we are forced to note that the substantial reduction in the American military presence has not stimulated any

decisive European process, far from it. Several of our partners have even begun considerably to reduce their armed forces and are placing themselves more than ever under American protection, incarnated through NATO. I draw the conclusion that if France wants to play a determining role in the creation of a European defense entity, she must take into account this state of mind of her partners, and reconsider to a large degree the form of her relations with NATO. It is clear in effect, that the necessary rebalancing of relations within the Atlantic Alliance, relying on existing European institutions such as the WEU, can only take place from the inside, not against the United States, but in agreement with her.[7]

None of the French leaders cited above called for a total reintegration of France into all NATO bodies and structures, but most agreed that France should participate more fully in NATO's political and military work, including perhaps the Defense Planning Committee (DPC) and the Nuclear Planning Group, both boycotted since 1966.

Since coming to power, the right has given some substance to these ideas and backed up Defense Minister François Léotard's claim to "want to work more with NATO on its new missions."[8] France, for example, took considerable advantage of NATO command assets for its peacekeeping engagement in Bosnia and Croatia, and French forces took full part in NATO's implementation of the no-fly zone over former Yugoslavia—the first NATO military mission ever executed.[9] France now also participates fully in NATO's Military Committee (military chiefs-of-staff), which it had partially boycotted since 1966, a step that became necessary when Paris agreed to a NATO role in an eventual implementation of the Vance-Owen Yugoslavia peace plan.[10] At the January 1994 NATO summit, France was the most active of all European countries in lobbying for greater U.S. involvement in former Yugoslavia, and it agreed not only to participate in a new NATO forum on nuclear non-proliferation but actually to co-chair the group along with the United States.[11] Both of these steps were unprecedented in the history of French-NATO affairs. The new French defense White Paper issued in early 1994—the first official outline of the underlying principles of French security policy since 1972—codified France's growing desire for closer cooperation with the United States and its NATO allies.[12]

There are, of course, limits to France's rapprochement with NATO, and those limits may be reached sooner than many Americans—and, indeed, Germans—hope. French officials, for example, continue to argue that NATO is excessively dominated by its military institutions and call for greater political control over the Supreme Allied Commander Europe (SACEUR, not coincidentally always an American so far) and the Defense Planning Committee. Some French diplomats have called the SACEUR "out of control" and see the DPC as having evolved into a sort of "second NATO Council."[13] France has also argued—setting it in conflict with the United States—that even where NATO takes responsibilities for peacekeeping missions, the United Nations Security Council (where France is one of five permanent members) should have the final say, not the North Atlantic Council (where France is one of sixteen). This dispute was particularly important in former Yugoslavia, where France continually refused—again in conflict with the United States—any NATO political role in any eventual implementation of a peace settlement. Whereas the United States insisted that an eventual peacekeeping force be placed under NATO command, France insisted that NATO's role be limited to that of executing decisions taken by the United Nations Security Council.[14] And even the new White Paper, it should be noted, makes clear that the evolutions of the past few years "do not . . . modify our particular military situation in NATO. The principles laid down in 1966 (non-participation in the integrated military command, full control over our forces and our territory, independence of our nuclear force, freedom to appraise the conditions of our security in time of crisis, freedom to choose our means in case of action) will continue to guide our relations with the integrated military command."[15]

Despite these difficulties and limits, evolving French attitudes toward NATO seem likely to continue and are a positive trend for the alliance as a whole. With France no longer opposed in principle to acting militarily within the NATO context even outside Europe, the alliance is better equipped to take on new roles in the post-Cold War world and avoid the irrelevance to which it would otherwise be fated. There is no guarantee that continued differences among the allies about NATO's future will be overcome or that the French rapprochement will go far enough to make a difference. But compared to the situation of 1990-1992, the evolution in France seems likely to contribute to a more coherent and effective Western alliance.

Continued Interest in a Prominent Global Role

France clearly remains committed to its traditional pursuit of a global security role. It has clung resolutely to its permanent UN Security Council seat and has been reluctant to welcome any new members; it has reiterated its commitment to remaining an independent nuclear power; and it has remained prepared to embark on high-profile or even spectacular national initiatives—such as Mitterrand's surprise visit to Sarajevo in June 1992, Dumas's threat to liberate prison camps in Bosnia alone if necessary, Mitterrand's calls for a nuclear conference of the four main nuclear powers, or Balladur's security pact.[16] As French policy in the Persian Gulf and Somalia demonstrated, moreover, France does not like to be left out of developments on the international stage. The Balladur government has continued to emphasize the importance of national grandeur and *rang* and no French government is likely to abandon France's special global ambitions.[17]

France's global commitment is more than just rhetorical or theatrical. It permanently deploys more than 25,000 troops in Africa, South America, and the South Pacific and maintains defense and security agreements with a number of countries in each region.[18] In addition and perhaps more importantly, throughout the early 1990s France deployed more peacekeepers around the world than any other country, including 4,800 in former Yugoslavia, 1,435 in Cambodia, 441 in South Lebanon, 30 in the Western Sahara, 20 in Iraq-Kuwait, 17 in Syria, and 16 in El Salvador.[19] The cost to France of these deployments in 1993 alone was FFr7 billion, of which only FFr1.5 billion would be reimbursed by the United Nations.[20] Since the end of the Cold War, the French defense budget has declined significantly more slowly than those of other Western powers, and funds for priorities like satellite intelligence and certain aspects of force projection have actually increased since 1989.[21] According to the new White Paper, the main gaps in French defense capabilities developed since the 1960s include weakness in intelligence systems, insufficient means of force projection, obsolete command systems, and deficiencies in allied interoperability—all necessary elements for a global military force.[22] There are obviously limits to the sort of global military role that France can play in a time of economic recession and budgetary severity, but it is clear that the will to devote resources to a prominent international security role is as strong in Paris as it is anywhere else in Europe.

Growing Preoccupation with Germany

German unification—the creation of a fully-sovereign Germany with an economy and population almost twice those of France—was in some ways a national trauma for which French leaders and public opinion were not prepared. Mitterrand's efforts to prevent or delay unification—his visits to Kiev and East Berlin in December 1989—and the later French Socialist strategy of binding the new Germany tightly into a European political, economic, and monetary union with a common defense all revealed a growing French preoccupation with its German neighbor and concern about how to "contain" it.[23] During the campaign for the referendum on the Maastricht treaty, the debate largely revolved around the issue of controlling Germany, with supporters of the treaty arguing that it would tie Germany down and opponents warning of German domination. Even proven friends of Germany found themselves playing to French fears of potential "anti-democratic ferment" and the "romantic, irrational forces in [Germany's] past."[24]

After coming to power in March 1993, the Balladur government was no less preoccupied with Germany than the Socialists, but it took a different approach toward its newly larger neighbor. Although divided between a highly federalist UDF led by former president Valéry Giscard d'Estaing and a more nationalist RPR led by Jacques Chirac (two-thirds of the RPR voted against the Maastricht treaty), the coalition government sought to play down the notion of diluting German power in a unified Europe and sought instead to maintain the relationship while augmenting the importance of other bilateral relationships. In RPR leader Jacques Chirac's words:

It's either one thing or the other: Either you are convinced, as I am, that Germany is and will remain democratic, that she has learned the lessons of history and in this case there is no reason to "contain" her; or you are convinced of the opposite, in which case no structure will resist German power but would on the contrary be dominated by it. If Germany must be "balanced," this will be done first and foremost by the economic recovery of France and not by the game of European institutions that would be unable to hide our weaknesses.[25]

Diplomatic advisers to Chirac such as Pierre Lellouche (who has since become an RPR member of parliament) and François Bujon de l'Estang also criticized the Socialists' efforts to "contain" Germany through institutions and announced (in the latter's words) that "the old federalist dream of a 'United States of Europe' is no longer relevant."[26] Balladur also criticized the Socialists for having "closed themselves up" in this "exclusive [Franco-German] game" and called on France to improve its ties with the United States and Great Britain.[27]

The "novelty" of this French approach, of course, should not be exaggerated, and Balladur has gone out of his way to show that the German relationship is still France's most important. He named a surprisingly "pro-European" government (including more UDF members than anticipated and excluding the leaders of the anti-Maastricht vote from foreign policy responsibilities), declared his commitment to the franc/mark parity within the European Monetary System's Exchange Rate Mechanism (ERM), and chose Bonn for his first foreign visit as prime minister, where he declared his conviction that "the future of Europe depends on the Franco-German couple."[28] In addition, the French public—like its German counterpart—still considers the Franco-German relationship solid and primordial. In a poll taken in late 1992, for example, 56 percent of the French believed Germany was their "most dependable ally" (compared to 42 percent who thought it was the United States), and 60 percent of French people called the Franco-German relationship either "unquestionable" or "solid" (compared to 37 percent who found it "fragile or threatened").[29] It is perhaps also worth noting that the French public was also more supportive of German unification than were French elites.[30]

Germany
Continued Support for NATO and the United States

Despite fears that a united Germany liberated from a direct military threat would turn away from its Cold War military alliance and allies, German leaders have continued to integrate their military forces in the West and have sought the maintenance of the military and nuclear support of the United States. After some hesitation during 1990-1991, the German public in both the eastern and western parts of the country has again become strongly in favor of a U.S. military presence in Germany, and German leaders have been among the leaders of Western efforts to reform NATO in order to keep it alive. Whereas in 1990, only 35 percent of Germans surveyed supported maintaining an American military presence in Germany and 53 percent favored a complete U.S. withdrawal, by 1992, 63 percent supported a residual American presence and only 39 percent favored full withdrawal. Two-thirds of the Germans polled in 1992 believed that NATO remains essential for German security (up from 58 percent in 1991), and nearly 75 percent of Germans viewed themselves as pro-American.[31]

Germany needs NATO and the United States today for the same reasons as during the Cold War, even if not as greatly as before. German leaders are well aware that the presence of American troops in Germany not only serves to deter any potential aggression and prevent the "nationalization" of European defense, but it also serves to reassure Germany's neighbors, who would be uncomfortable without the Americans around. Committed to nonnuclear status, Germans feel more comfortable with an American nuclear guarantee and are still not ready to accept such a guarantee from France—which is not being offered anyway.[32] Many Germans appear to accept the French thesis that the American role in Europe is bound to decline, but they believe this means they should seek to counter that process, not help it along. It is not unimportant, finally, that most Germans see the United States as the only Western country that supported unification without reservations.[33]

There is also much continuity in Germany's effort to balance its NATO relationship with its resolve to pursue security integration with France within Europe. For each German commitment to NATO (such as integration into the Rapid Reaction Corps or the sponsoring of the North Atlantic Cooperation Council (NACC), for example, Germany has taken commensurate steps to satisfy France (such as the creation of the Eurocorps and the proposals on the European security identity). This traditional German balancing between French and American positions has been a highly successful strategy that Germany will doubtless pursue as long as possible. As Foreign Minister Kinkel put it: "We cannot accept an 'either-or' situation."[34]

A Growing Global Security Role

Germany's attitude toward and role in security beyond Western Europe has been changing since unification. As recently as 1990, for example, when the Persian Gulf War broke out, Germany was still marked by its Cold War reticence and ambivalence toward military force, and it failed to show much interest in adopting a more prominent international security role. Since the Gulf War, however (and partly because of it), Germany's external security policy has gradually changed and its willingness to adopt new responsibilities has grown. By the end of 1993, Germany had deployed minesweepers in the Persian Gulf (breaking with the "out-of-area" precedent), sent a small number of troops to Iran to help bring assistance to threatened Kurds, dispatched military sanitation and medical officers to the UN deployment in Cambodia, played a major role in the airborne surveillance of the international embargo on Serbia (manning over 30 percent of the AWACS flights involved), sent armed soldiers to Somalia to help with the delivery of humanitarian assistance, and participated actively in the airlift of food and medical supplies to Sarajevo and other parts of Bosnia. The Kohl government has pushed for the removal of some restrictions on the use of German military forces abroad and, after some hesitation, began publicly to seek a permanent UN Security Council seat.[35] In early 1994, the German defense ministry produced its own "white paper," which called for the creation of rapid reaction forces capable of taking part in all sorts of United Nations military contingencies.[36]

The German government's expressed desire to play a greater international role seems increasingly to be supported by German public opinion. A majority of Germans, for example, now believe that the Federal Republic should assume a more active international role (62 percent); that their country is best equipped to lead a European foreign policy (77 percent); that Germany should participate in peacekeeping operations (53 percent); and that the principle of intervention, including military intervention, is justified in support of international law or human rights (53 percent, up from 43 percent in 1991).[37] In addition, whereas until the late 1980s a majority of Germans believed that the past prohibited Germans from participating in (even UN-sponsored) military actions abroad, by early 1993 only 31 percent opposed German participation, with 50 percent agreeing that Germany should participate "exactly as England, France or the Americans."[38] Even in the opposition SPD, leading foreign policy experts have begun to call for the "end of [German] provincialism" and to support German participation in UN peacekeeping operations.[39] West Germany's Cold War reticence was based on factors—such as the legacy of the past and the Soviet threat—that have diminished over the years and especially since 1989. As a result, German security policy is likely to become more global, less reticent, and less averse to military means than in the past.[40]

One should be careful, of course, not to exaggerate how far Germany has come up until now or the potential for rapid change; significant constraints on a global German security role remain in place. First, the memory of World War II has not disappeared within Germany or in neighboring states, and even the Kohl government continues to argue that Germany cannot deploy military forces in states where the *Wehrmacht* was used.[41] Second, despite the green light given by the Federal Constitutional Court to all of Germany's foreign troop deployments so far, legal restrictions—or at least complications—remain on the use of German military forces abroad. The SPD continues to refuse the constitutional amendments proposed by the government that would permit peacemaking and peacekeeping, and the CDU's coalition partner Federal Democratic Party (FDP) will not countenance such actions without a constitutional change.[42] Third, public opinion, while apparently changing, remains reticent: If a majority support the *principle* of military intervention or UN operations, only 32 percent of those polled supported Bundeswehr participation in NATO operations outside Germany, and only 20 percent supported German military participation in UN-sponsored operations like those in the Persian Gulf.[43] No less than 31 percent (40 percent in the FDP, 34 percent in the SPD, and only 21 percent in the CDU) "approve of the solution that we support [UN military actions] financially but do not participate ourselves."[44] Fourth, given the costs of unification and the pressures for defense cuts, it seems unlikely that Bonn will devote significant means to developing the sorts of force projection and intelligence capabilities that would be necessary to develop autonomous European or Franco-German military forces. Finally, there are political barriers to a greater German international security role: Despite a gradual trend since 1990 toward acceptance of the potential need for the use of military force and the potential need for German participation, the SPD recently made it clear that it would only support German participation in UN peacekeeping operations that were clearly limited to peacekeeping, and it strictly rejected German participation in peacemaking or other military interventions.[45] According to SPD manager Günter Verheugen, German armed forces "cannot be used for wars . . . that have nothing to do with the defense of our country."[46] It will be a long time before German attitudes about their global security role begin to closely resemble those of France.

Declining Relative Interest in France

Abundant evidence is available that Germany still sees France as its primary partner. In the 1992 *Le Monde* poll previously mentioned, for example, 52 percent of the Germans asked considered France their most dependable ally (with, significantly, only 35 percent saying it was the United States), and 71 percent of Germans found their relationship with France to be "unquestionable" or "solid," with only 24 percent believing otherwise.[47] The German government on many occasions has also expressed its continued commitment to the special relationship—as seen in the numerous joint proposals on political union, the agreement to monetary union, the creation of the Eurocorps, and others—that it considers the Franco-German relationship a foreign policy priority. In keeping with historical patterns of Germany managing its relations with both France and the United States, Chancellor Kohl has continued to make it clear—for example by standing by France's refusal to accept the November 1992 EC-U.S. "Blair House" agricultural agreement—that he will not easily turn his back on France.[48]

At the same time, however, there is reason to believe that Germany will be less willing than in the past to compromise its own direct interests simply in order to maintain good relations with France. Throughout the postwar era, Germany needed strong ties with France in order to help restore its lost democratic legitimacy, to ensure France's commitment to German security against the Russian threat, and to foster the development of a European community without which it was difficult for Germany to act. West Germany was also prosperous enough to compensate its neighbor financially—for example in the EC's common agricultural policy—in order to preserve the strength of the bilateral tie. At present, however, Germany arguably not only needs France less than it did during the Cold War but—with huge budget deficits, trade deficits and spending of more than DM 150 billion per year on reconstruction of the five new German states (*Länder*)—it may be led to drive a harder bargain in dealing with its closest partner. In addition, a new generation of German leaders born after World War II may not have the same sense of the historic mission of Franco-German reconciliation as have had all German chancellors from Adenauer down to his protege Helmut Kohl. Finally, as already seen, Germany also has new interests and responsibilities in the East that can only distract it from its dealings in the West.

Has there been any indication so far that Germany has downgraded its relations with France or that it will at least drive a harder bargain with it? While few Germans would go as far as former FDP leader Otto Graf Lambsdorff in saying that "the German economy is more important than the quality of our relations with France," other German officials have made it clear that severe economic pressures at home and increasing obligations abroad may make them less inclined or able to give foreign policy priority to France.[49] Foreign Minister Kinkel, for example—has reminded the French that "solidarity is a two-way street," Finance Minister Theo Waigel bluntly declared that if the European Central Bank is not in Frankfurt there will not be one at all, and Chancellor Kohl himself has now insisted that if and when Germany receives a permanent U.N. Security Council seat it should come with full veto rights like those of Britain and France.[50] France is still the priority, but it may be forced in the future to occupy a lower place on a very crowded German agenda.[51]

Notes

[1] For some arguments to this effect, see David S. Yost, "France in the New Europe," *Foreign Affairs* 69, no. 5 (winter 1990-1991):107-128.

[2] The decisions on NATO peacekeeping were taken at the Oslo ministerial conference (for CSCE in June 1992) and Brussels ministerial conference (for the UN in December 1992). For Oslo, see Claire Tréan, "L'Alliance atlantique pourrait

intervenir pour des missions de maintien de la paix en Europe," *Le Monde*, June 5, 1992, p. 4. For Brussels, see "Europeans Reach a Peacekeeping Accord as France Yields," *International Herald Tribune*, December 19-20, 1992, p. 2, in which a NATO official is cited as saying "The French finally gave in." The official texts are the NATO communiqué of June 4, 1992. For Brussels, see the NATO communiqué of December 17, 1992. For Joxe's position, see his opening speech to a colloquium on defense in Paris, published as "Discours d'ouverture," in *Un nouveau débat stratégique*, actes du colloque de Paris, September 29-30, October 1, 1992, pp. 7-8. Also see David Buchan, "Joxe Urges Bigger French Role in Nato," *Financial Times*, September 30, 1992.

[3] For Mitterrand's critique, see Claire Tréan, "M. Mitterrand a dénoncé le 'prêchi-prêcha' de l'OTAN," *Le Monde*, November 10-11, 1991. For Dumas, see Claire Tréan, "La relation de la France à l'OTAN n'est pas modifiée, *Le Monde*, March 23, 1991. Also see Dumas's comments in "L'élargissement des compétences de l'OTAN continue d'alimenter la polémique entre Français et Américains," *Le Monde*, June 6, 1992, p. 4; and "Roland Dumas contre une Europe des technocrates," *Libération*, December 6, 1991, p. 18. French opposition to NATO reform during 1990-1992 is discussed in Philip H. Gordon, *French Security Policy After the Cold War: Continuity, Change and Implications for the United States*, R-4229-A (Santa Monica, CA: RAND, 1992), pp. 9-20.

[4] See "Un entretien avec M. Alain Juppé," *Le Monde*, March 6, 1993, p. 7.

[5] For Chirac's quote, see his February 26, 1992, speech at the Institut de France, "Contradictions et convergences dans les relations franco-allemandes depuis la chute du mur de Berlin," p. 13, text provided by office of Jacques Chirac. For Lellouche, see Pierre Lellouche, "Pour une nouvelle donne franco-allemande," *Le Monde*, February 24, 1993; and the four-part series by Lellouche, "La France, l'OTAN et le Nouveau Monde," *Le Figaro*, July 18-26, 1992.

[6] Baumel asked: "Can France send its Rapid Action Force in an important intervention independently from NATO, i.e. the Americans, without having dealt with problems of intelligence, logistics and air support? The answer is no.... Since it is obvious that from the first shot in any large military action our forces will be placed without reservations under NATO command, as happened in the Gulf with the American headquarters, why be absent today from the organisms in which the nature of the missions as well as the modalities of intervention of these forces are discussed and decided in advance?" See Jacques Baumel, "La France, l'OTAN et les Etats-Unis," *Le Monde*, April 1, 1993, p. 2. For Bujon de l'Estang, see his "Time for a New French Foreign Policy," *Wall Street Journal Europe*, March 30, 1993.

[7] See Chirac's February 8, 1993, speech at a reception in honor of Parisian reserve officers, cited in the symposium report by Robert P. Grant, *The Changing Franco-American Security Relationship: New Directions for NATO and European Defense Cooperation* (Arlington, VA: U.S.-CREST, December 1993), remarks translated by Grant.

[8] See "M. Léotard: Paris veut 'travailler davantage' avec l'OTAN sur ses 'missions nouvelles,'" Agence France Presse, Informations générales, August 25, 1993.

[9] See Joseph Fitchett, "NATO Will Use Jets in Bosnia to Protect UN's Peace Troops," *International Herald Tribune*, July 15, 1993.

[10] French representatives had been present at Military Committee meetings even after the 1966-1967 withdrawal, but as observers with no more than a "consultative" voice—they could intervene when asked questions but did not participate fully in debates. Reasoning that NATO was now involved with French participation in the "no-fly" zone in Yugoslavia and that it might participate in peacekeeping missions elsewhere, France decided to begin taking full part in Military Committee meetings where such interventions would be planned. Since April 1993, France has had a full "deliberative" voice at Military Committee meetings (interviews in Paris, June 1993). Also see Jacques Isnard, "La France siège désormais avec voix délibérative au comité militaire de l'OTAN," *Le Monde*, May 14, 1993, p. 5.

[11] Interviews with U.S. officials in Washington, DC, February 1994.

[12] See Ministère de la Défense, *Livre Blanc sur la Défense, 1994* (Paris: Service d'Information et de Relations Publiques des Armées, Ministère de la Défense, 1994), pp. 34-37. The White Paper specifically states (p. 37) that it is now "logical to ensure French participation in the meetings of NATO decision-making bodies whenever the engagement of French forces or interests is in question. The presence of the defense minister, at the [North] Atlantic Council, in addition to that of the foreign minister and that of the chief of staff of the armed forces at the Military Committee, shall henceforth be decided on a case-by-case basis by the President of the Republic and the prime minister."

[13] This critique was widespread among sources interviewed in Paris during 1993, including in the relatively "pro-NATO" French defense ministry. For a published critique of the DPC's allegedly excessive political power, see G. Trangis (pseudonym), "Ni splendide isolement ni réintégration," *Le Monde*, July 14, 1993, p. 2.

[14] Interviews in Paris, 1992-1993. Also see, "Qui commandera la force de l'OTAN chargée de faire applique le plan de paix?" *Le Monde*, March 13, 1993, p. 4; and Michael R. Gordon, "U.S. and France at Odds over A Bosnia Force," *International Herald Tribune*, March 12, 1993.

[15] Ministère de la Défense, *Livre Blanc*, pp. 36-37.

[16] On the Sarajevo visit, see William Drozdiak, "Cheers at Home, Restraint Abroad for Mitterrand," *Washington Post*, June 30, 1992, p. A13. For Dumas, see "M. Roland Dumas suggère que la France libère 'par la force' les camps de détention de Bosnie," *Le Monde*, January 12, 1993. On the continued French pursuit of international prominence in general, see Alan Riding, "France Is Seeking More Global Clout," *International Herald Tribune*, June 28, 1993, p. 5.

[17] See Balladur's assertion that he "completely believes in the idea that France must, whenever it can, play a leading role in international affairs . . . that is one of the justifications of its role as a permanent member of the Security Council"

(cited in "Un entretien avec Edouard Balladur," *Le Monde*, May 18, 1993, p. 8).

[18] For a list of the main countries with French deployments and the numbers and types of soldiers there, see International Institute for Strategic Studies (IISS), *The Military Balance 1993-1994* (London: IISS/Brassey's, October 1993), pp. 44-45.

[19] See *ibid.* as well as the charts provided in "Dix mille soldats français engagés dans le monde," *Le Monde*, December 12, 1992, p. 3.

[20] See David Buchan and Reuter Press Agency, "Balladur settles feud on defence," *Financial Times*, March 16, 1994, p. 2.

[21] The French defense budget fell 0.1 percent in 1991, 2.6 percent in 1992, and 2.8 percent in 1993. For Germany, the figures are -7.3, -4.5, and -6.5; for Britain they are +5.8, -4.1, and -17; and for the U.S. -3.7, -4.4 and -3.4. See IISS, *The Military Balance 1993-1994*, pp. 20, 41, and 45. On the new French priorities within the French defense budget, see Gordon, *French Security Policy After the Cold War*, pp. 39-42.

[22] See Ministère de la Défense, *Livre Blanc*, p. 5.

[23] For a discussion of France's concerns about German unification and Mitterrand's efforts to delay it, see Julius W. Friend, *The Linchpin: French-German Relations, 1950-1990*, The Washington Papers, no. 154 (Washington DC: Praeger/Center for Strategic and International Studies, 1991), pp. 78-89. Also see Ingo Kolboom, *Vom geteilten zum vereinten Deutschland: Deutschland-Bilder in Frankreich*, Arbeitspapiere zur internationalen Politik, no. 61 (Bonn: Forschungsinstitut der Deutschen Gesellschaft für Auswärtige Politik, April 1991).

[24] The first quote is from then-prime minister Pierre Bérégovoy, the second from Michel Rocard. For the citations and on the use of negative images of Germany during the French referendum campaign, see William Drozdiak, "Old Fears of Germany Surface in French Debate on Maastricht," *International Herald Tribune*, September 1, 1992, p. 1.

[25] See Chirac's February 26, 1992, speech at the Institut de France, "Contradictions et convergences dans les relations franco-allemandes depuis la chute du mur de Berlin," text provided by office of Jacques Chirac.

[26] See Lellouche, "Pour une nouvelle donne franco-allemande;" and François Bujon de l'Estang, "Time for a New French Foreign Policy."

[27] Balladur wrote that "without abandoning the special Franco-German relationship, we must not close ourselves up in this exclusive game. France, whose vocation is not only European, can—while conserving her good relations with Germany—improve those that she has with the United States and Great Britain." See Edouard Balladur, "Le monde change, il faut changer la politique aussi: La France et le nouvel ordre planétaire," *Le Figaro*, February 2, 1992, p. 6.

[28] In the Balladur government, former president of the European Parliament Simone Veil was named first minister of state (the number two position in the government), one anti-Maastricht leader (Charles Pasqua) was named to the interior ministry rather than defense as he reportedly wished, and the other (Philippe

Séguin) was kept out of the government altogether, taking on the position of speaker of the National Assembly. On Balladur's visit to Bonn, see "Balladur setzt auf Bonn," *Süddeutsche Zeitung*, April 10-12, 1993.

[29] See the poll and commentary in Luc Rosenzweig, "Un mariage de raison plutôt qu'une passion folle," *Le Monde*, January 23, 1993, p. 7.

[30] See Kolboom, *Vom geteilten zum vereinten Deutschland.*

[31] For data, see the series of polls sponsored by the RAND Corporation and conducted with Infratest Burke Berlin in Ronald D. Asmus, *Germany in Transition: National Self-Confidence and International Reticence*, N-3352-AF (Santa Monica, CA: RAND, 1992); and Ronald D. Asmus, "Germany's Geopolitical Maturation: Strategy and Public Opinion After the Wall," *RAND Issue Paper* (Santa Monica, CA: RAND, February 1993).

[32] In early 1992, President Mitterrand and certain defense ministry officials made some highly public statements about possibly developing a "European nuclear doctrine," and preliminary discussions began later that year between the French, British, Germans, and other Europeans about what such a doctrine might look like. As of early 1994, the discussions had not gone very far, however, and Defense Minister Léotard made it clear that "the industrial and technological means directly tied to nuclear deterrence must remain the exclusive domain of national competence." On the broaching of a "European nuclear doctrine," see Gordon, *French Security Policy After the Cold War*, pp. 26-27. For Léotard see "Contestant la thèse des 'dividendes de la paix' M. Léotard estime qu'il y aurait un grave risque à se lancer dans un désarmement budgétaire," *Le Monde*, September 10, 1993.

[33] A high-ranking German politician closely involved in the unification process told me that he would never forget the role played by George Bush and the Americans during unification, and that "the role of certain other Western leaders was not as supportive." Asked to be more specific, the politician simply repeated that "the role of other Western leaders was not as supportive" (interview in Bonn, May 1993). On American support for German unification, also see Steven F. Szabo, *The Diplomacy of German Unification* (New York: St. Martin's Press, 1993).

[34] See "Bonn und Paris wollen den Weg in die Zukunft weisen," *Frankfurter Allgemeine Zeitung*, January 22, 1993.

[35] See Rick Atkinson, "Bonn Presses for Lead UN Role," *Washington Post*, September 27, 1993, p. A14.

[36] See German Ministry of Defense, *Weißbuch 1994 zur Sicherheit der Bundesrepublik Deutschland und zur Lage und Zukunft der Bundeswehr* (Bonn: Bundesverteidigungsministerium, 1994).

[37] On recent public opinion trends in Germany where international affairs are concerned, see Asmus, "Germany's Geopolitical Maturation;" and Renate Köcher, "Breite Mehrheit für Blauhelm-Einsätze deutscher Soldaten," *Frankfurter Allgemeine Zeitung*, February 11, 1993, p. 5.

[38] See Köcher, "Breite Mehrheit," p. 5.

[39] The call for an end of "provincialism" was from SPD defense expert Karsten

Voigt in "Für Kampfeinsätze der Bundeswehr," *Süddeutsche Zeitung*, February 4, 1993. On individual SPD support for UN peacekeeping and even peacemaking initiatives, also see "Klose fordert von der SPD neue Beschlüsse zu Kampfeinsätzen," *Frankfurter Allgemeine Zeitung*, July 1, 1993, p. 1; and "Verheugen: SPD muß ihre Haltung ändern," *Frankfurter Allgemeine Zeitung*, September 8, 1993.

⁴⁰ For an analysis of the factors that limited Germany's foreign policy in the past and how that foreign policy might be changing today, see Philip H. Gordon, "The Normalization of German Foreign Policy," *Orbis* 38, no. 2 (spring 1994):225-243.

⁴¹ See the discussion of Kohl's statement to this effect at the annual Munich Security Policy Conference (formerly Wehrkunde) in Josef Joffe, "Übrig bleibt die Allianz," *Süddeutsche Zeitung*, February 8, 1993. As Joffe points out, this constraint is obviously highly restrictive given the expanse of German military actions during World War II.

⁴² For SPD opposition, see "Zweifel in der SPD am Parteitagsbeschluß zu Blauhelmen," *Frankfurter Allgemeine Zeitung*, August 10, 1993; and "Das SPD-Präsidium verwirft Kloses Vorstellungen von einer deutschen Beteiligung bei UN-Einsätzen," *Frankfurter Allgemeine Zeitung*, August 25, 1993.

⁴³ See Asmus, "Germany's Geopolitical Maturation," p. 3.

⁴⁴ See Köcher, "Breite Mehrheit," p. 5.

⁴⁵ The party defined peacekeeping (as opposed to peacemaking) as operations that "had the fundamental agreement of the parties to the conflict . . . were strictly neutral vis-à-vis parties to the conflict . . . [included] the participation of civilian, police and military personnel as part of the overall concept of peacekeeping and [involved] the open presence of UN soldiers with rules on the use of weapons as restrictive as possible." See "SPD-Vorschlag zur Beteiligung Deutschlands an UN-Einsätzen," *Frankfurter Allgemeine Zeitung*, August 25, 1993.

⁴⁶ Verheugen cited in Rick Atkinson, "New 'Grand Coalition' Less Likely in Germany," *Washington Post*, August 25, 1993.

⁴⁷ See Rosenzweig, "Un mariage de raison plutôt qu'une passion folle," p. 7. When asked in a separate poll who their best ally would be "in a crisis," the German choice between France and the United States was reversed, with about half choosing Washington and 30 percent saying it was Paris. See Rick Atkinson, "Americans Fear Nazism Is Reviving, Poll Finds," *Washington Post*, September 8, 1993.

⁴⁸ After a two-hour meeting with Balladur intended to overcome recent Franco-German tensions over monetary policy and trade, Kohl signaled his willingness to support France's position in the transatlantic dispute, declaring there were "enormous problems with the agricultural part" of the Uruguay round of trade negotiations. See Rick Atkinson, "Kohl Shores Up France in Trade Dispute with U.S.," *Washington Post*, August 27, 1993.

⁴⁹ Lambsdorff cited in "Chauvin was a Frenchman," *The Economist*, March 20, 1993, p. 53.

[50] Kinkel is cited in Tom Heneghan, "Franco-German Meetings to Put Tandem Back on Track," Reuters Press Agency, August 22, 1993. On the canceled meeting of finance ministers, see Roger Cohen, "Bonn to Paris: We're Still in Charge," *International Herald Tribune*, June 25, 1993, pp. 1, 12. For Kohl on the UN veto, see "Kohl macht deutlich: In den Sicherheitsrat nur mit Veto-Recht," *Süddeutsche Zeitung*, July 10, 1993, p. 1.

[51] On potential impatience with France in German public opinion, see analyst Angelika Volle's comment, "It has dawned on the man in the street that, if Europe is only in the interest of the French, then he is not very happy with it" (cited in Heneghan, "Franco-German Meetings to Put Tandem Back on Track").

4

Conclusions: The Franco-German Partnership and the Western Alliance

One of the main hypotheses at the start of this study was that Franco-German security cooperation would become more difficult in the post-Cold War era; the analysis of the first few years of that era confirms that assessment. With the Cold War no longer in place to harmonize their interests, France and Germany had great difficulties forging common security policies toward European security institutions and in Yugoslavia. They played very different roles in the Persian Gulf War and have developed structurally dissimilar interests in Central and Eastern Europe. While there seems to have been some convergence on attitudes toward NATO (France moving toward Germany) and on the question of joint security policies outside Europe (Germany moving toward France), favorable government attitudes and policies in each country toward the other probably have not been strengthened by the events of the past few years. Potentially even more important, a Germany freed from past constraints and under great new demands may be obliged to place other foreign policy priorities above its traditional relationship with France, which could conceivably trigger French efforts to obstruct German goals.

Notwithstanding these problems and dangers, pessimistic predictions of the end of Franco-German cooperation in the post-Cold War world seem highly exaggerated. The new Franco-German security relationship may be less natural than the old and it will doubtless experience periodic tensions and failures, but it is likely to endure for at least three main reasons.

First—and this is the flaw in the "structural-realist" view—both governments know they still need each other. The postwar Franco-German special relationship has been the result of each country pursuing its own national self-interests through cooperation rather than conflict with the other, and there is no reason this calculus of interests should now change. France and Germany now account for more than one-tenth of each other's external trade, are manifestly interdependent in monetary affairs, and are more affected than ever by each other's problems through the EC's single market and open frontiers. Given such stakes in each other's fate, it seems unlikely that France and Germany would ever let external developments come between them. While crises such as the situation in former Yugoslavia have shown the potential for real disagreement, it is hard to imagine what external issue could seem more important to Bonn or Paris than their relations with each other. Indeed, it is worth noting that the conflict in Yugoslavia did *not* lead to Franco-German hostility, as it almost certainly would have in previous eras.

Second, if it is true, as argued here, that Germany now needs France less than it did before, it would be a great mistake to conclude that Germany will feel free to ignore its primary European partner. German foreign policy may no longer operate under some of the constraints of the past, but it remains highly dependent on the support and cooperation of its neighbors and allies. Germans remain particularly sensitive to the way their foreign policies are perceived abroad and will continue to go out of their way to convince their neighbors that Germany is permanently and concretely integrated in its European and Atlantic alliances, and in particular, with its former adversary, France. The assertiveness German leaders displayed in the recognition of Croatia and Slovenia was to a certain extent an aberration, and the reaction it brought about has served as a reminder of how problematic a unilateral or national German foreign policy would be. Germany's international caution since its recognition of Croatia and Slovenia suggests that consideration of or even deference to allies' interests and views will remain a core characteristic of German foreign policy.

Third, and most important, there seems to be strong evidence of what might be called a Franco-German "partnership prejudice"—a bias toward bilateral cooperation for cooperation's sake and a desire to do everything possible to avoid both the impression and the existence of divergence. Indeed, the case studies undertaken in Chapter 2 demonstrate how the two countries often approached international security problems or crises with divergent positions but followed that divergence with extraordinary efforts to harmonize their policies. Rather than drive the two countries apart, crises actually seem to bring France and Germany closer together. The response to tensions over unification, for example, was not divorce but bilateral proposals for a "European political union." The early debates over the reform of European security institutions ended with fundamental agreement (Germany's decision to integrate into NATO's Rapid Reaction Corps and multinational corps was soon compensated by the announcement of the Franco-German corps). The initially divergent reactions to the Gulf War ended with both France and Germany fully supporting the American-led coalition and with calls to develop Europe's own security identity. And even in former Yugoslavia, where cooperation has proved most difficult, both countries have modified their preferred policies in order not to alienate the other. The basic reasons France and Germany chose to integrate with each other in the first place—to overcome past enmity, to augment their prosperity, to combine their means for a greater voice in the world, and to dilute German power—still hold. Economic crises, domestic politics, and Europe's new geopolitical arrangement will make the partnership more difficult than it has been since the early 1950s but are unlikely to break it apart.

The biggest problem with the Franco-German security relationship is, thus, not so much keeping the two countries together but giving the partnership substance and translating a general will to cooperate into a more effective contribution to European and Atlantic security. As seen in this study, security cooperation between the two countries has not yet developed into the capability to act as a decisive and coherent unit in the international security domain. And what, ultimately, is the goal of the Franco-German partnership beyond the symbolic reconciliation of the two countries, which seems to have been already achieved? Is Franco-German partnership not also meant to contribute more broadly to European and international security, and if it is, what is the logic of doing so on a bilateral rather than an international basis? Is there not a danger that by coming together bilaterally, France and Germany will tend to weaken their other, broader European and Atlantic alliances?

Such questions have legitimately been raised by all of France and Germany's allies. Within Europe, there is still resentment about Franco-German tendencies to "go it alone," and many of the smaller states are concerned about domination by their larger French and German partners. One can legitimately ask why France and Germany should have their own bilateral commissions, treaties, or military forces, why bilateral arms production should be a priority over multilateral ones, and why France and Germany should feel free to make their own bilateral proposals for European political or economic union without involving the EC as a whole. On the Atlantic side, similar questions arise, and it was no secret that many Americans felt slighted by Franco-German attempts to endow the European Community with a defense identity and, more specifically, to create the Eurocorps. Historically, Americans have supported Franco-German and European security cooperation when it has seemed to mean better burden-sharing or when it meant stronger defense against the Soviet Union.[1] But as noted previously, Americans wonder about the true goals of bilateral security cooperation that could make the United States redundant as a European power.

These problems are genuine and have to do with more than national pride. Surely, Europe would be better off if foreign and security policy were decided among the Twelve, and any bilateral Franco-German efforts are bound to have less support, less legitimacy, and less means behind them than policies supported by the European Community as a whole. Moreover, even when the Community does manage to reach a consensus, it remains questionable whether even a unified Europe can take effective action without the United States. Indeed, the past several years seem to suggest that Europe still needs American leadership and resources, especially (but not only) where the military arena is concerned. In the Gulf War, the Middle East peace process, the organization of aid to Russia, and even in the humanitarian intervention in Somalia—American leadership, decisiveness, and/or military power seemed necessary to bring about results. In former Yugoslavia, where the initial American reaction was to leave the crisis in Europe's hands, neither leadership, decisiveness, nor sufficient military means to resolve the conflict were displayed. This does not imply that American leadership could have provided a solution in Yugoslavia, but it does suggest that decisive leadership is even more unlikely when the United States is not involved. So long as there are historical and political constraints on German armed forces, moreover, questions about the seriousness of Franco-German military cooperation will remain. In certain regards, France's natural European partner is not Germany but Great Britain.

Despite all of these problems, Franco-German security cooperation remains important and, on balance, positive for Europe, the Atlantic alliance, and the international system. For a number of reasons, France and Germany should continue to pursue common security policies and common means of implementing them, even when it means moving ahead of their partners and allies.

First, as preferable as it would be for the European Union as a whole (and not just Paris and Bonn) to make foreign policy, a true common foreign and security policy made by the twelve diverse states of the EU is simply unlikely, a problem that will become even greater when the Union is enlarged. We have already seen here the difficulties in reaching common views and implementing common policies by two neighboring countries who have worked for forty years to develop their security policy cooperation, and it seems implausible that this will be easier or even possible among 15 or 20 European countries. The Maastricht agreement on a "common foreign and security policy" was no more than a vague commitment to try where possible to cooperate, and it will be difficult in the future to reconcile the interests of countries from Portugal to Sweden and from Poland to Greece.

To the extent that the EU will need common security policies and the means to implement them, moreover, history suggests that Franco-German cooperation can set an example and provide the impetus to further integration. Other European institutions—such as the European Coal and Steel Community (1952), the European Economic Community (1958), and the European Monetary System (1979)—began largely as Franco-German initiatives; all initially excluded certain European states, and all eventually attracted the other states as their success became apparent. There seems to be reason to hope that if France and Germany seek to harmonize their own positions and develop bilateral political and military instruments, other European states will be prompted to join--as Belgium has already done with the Eurocorps. Europe's structural flaw is that—unlike the Atlantic alliance during the Cold War—it does not have a natural leader. A decisive Franco-German core—if it could show the ability to reach common decisions and could deploy the means to implement them—could arguably help Europe become a more credible international actor.

Moreover, where the Atlantic connection is concerned, there does seem to be a certain logic for Western Europe—with 345 million inhabitants, the world's largest market, and proximity to three of the world's most unstable regions (North Africa, Eastern Europe, and the Middle East)—to have its own means and options available to it if the United States should prove unwilling or unable to act. Diplomatically, there is no reason that Europe should not be able to define its own interests and call on its peoples to support them, for example, in organizing democratization programs in Central Europe, in controlling the proliferation of advanced weapons in North Africa, in delivering aid to the former Soviet Union, or in controlling the spread of war in the Balkans. With limited means and potentially divergent priorities, the United States may not always be willing to act in those areas that Europeans find necessary. This, after all, is what a high-ranking State Department official declared not long after the Clinton administration took office, and the impression that domestic priorities have become most important in the United States has yet to be disproved by U.S. actions abroad.[2]

Bilateral Franco-German cooperation, moreover, is also important to the two countries' own relationship in that it helps to bind their interests together. If a situation were allowed to develop (as in many ways it already has) in which Germany were to take near-exclusive responsibility for stability and security in Eastern Europe, whereas France alone dealt with North Africa, national interests in each region would become even more divergent than history and geography presently render them. With divergent interests and stakes in different regions, sudden crises in those regions could easily lead to serious divisions between Paris and Bonn.

What is true of the political-diplomatic domain is even more true of the military one. At present, Europe is simply incapable of taking large-scale military action without the United States. It lacks the satellite and intelligence capabilities to determine what is happening in areas of regional tension, the logistic and projection capabilities to deploy major forces abroad, a credible autonomous nuclear deterrent for the EU as a whole, and the experience and organized command structures that would be necessary to take decisive military action. With the United States in the process of withdrawing troops from Europe, severely cutting back its military forces, and redefining its interests and commitments abroad, it cannot be taken for granted that the United States will always be ready, willing, or able to play a military role in the defense of European interests.

As early U.S. policy in the Yugoslav crisis demonstrates, there are cases of vital interest to Europe in which the United States may decide not to get involved. Unless one can forever exclude the potential necessity of using military force in Europe or elsewhere, a certain degree of autonomous European capabilities seems desirable. And regardless of whether one believes that a large-scale military intervention in former Yugoslavia would have been useful or advisable, it seems at least clear that military peacekeeping, logistical, intelligence, and deterrent forces played a major role there even in the absence of such an intervention. Even if one believes that it would be far more desirable for Europe to exercise any eventual military action together with the United States—and this is the position of the author—it can be argued that the costs of developing and maintaining such military forces should be shared between Europe and the United States more equally than is presently the case. (Despite the recent cuts, the U.S.

military budget is still 4.8 percent of U.S. GDP, whereas the British figure is down to 4.0 percent, the French 2.7 percent, and the German 1.9 percent).[3] The sort of "division of labor" in which Europe makes foreign policy with financial means and the United States with military means would lead to the same type of problematic division of interests and risks that a Franco-German regional division of labor would produce.

Viewed objectively, strictly bilateral Franco-German security policy cooperation is not an optimal arrangement. The advantages of a political community of two are obviously valid in communities of twelve, sixteen, or twenty-five as well. But optimal solutions are not always available in a complicated world of diverse nation-states and, until more multilateral solutions become available, it would seem unwise to hold back on Franco-German cooperation while waiting for something better to come along in its place. The problems with bilateral Franco-German security cooperation is not that it has gone too far too fast but that it has not gone far enough.

The challenge to French and German leaders in the coming decade, then, is to find a way to pursue their bilateral cooperation without detracting from broader European and Atlantic cooperation. This they can do vis-à-vis their European allies by opening up their bilateral integration–as with the Eurocorps–to any EC partner that wants to join, provided that the partner is genuinely committed to the common goal. The European states that want to join should be integrated and those that do not can remain outside. If all aspects of Franco-German security cooperation—such as the joint brigade or the Elysée Treaty—cannot be opened up to other states for symbolic reasons, France and Germany should at least seek to involve other states in their deliberations and try to avoid surprise announcements like the Eurocorps.

In the Atlantic domain, more transparency and general demonstrations of good will are required. Americans—especially to the extent that they withdraw from their Cold War international leadership position to focus on domestic affairs–should understand Europe's natural desire to develop its own capacity and identity in the diplomatic and military areas. Why should Europe *not* seek to enhance its leverage and make sure its specific interests are being ensured on the world stage? But Americans will not, and should not, understand if Franco-German or European cooperation seems to be an attempt to take advantage of the U.S. presence as a last-resort military force while freezing it out of European security discussions and plans. Paris and Bonn should make it clear that, if made available in the name of common transatlantic interests, American participation or even leadership will be welcomed. Franco-German security cooperation, if used as a tool to lead and further integrate the other European countries and to share more equitably the burdens and responsibilities with the United States, can contribute to a more secure, more integrated, and more stable world.

Notes

[1] This point is well demonstrated in Anne Engels, "Die USA und der Europäische Pfeiler 1984-92: WEU und deutsch-französische Sicherheitskooperation aus amerikanischer Sicht," unpublished master's thesis, Bonn University, 1993.

[2] According to Deputy Secretary of State Peter Tarnoff, the third ranking official at the State Department, "It is necessary to make the point that our economic interests are paramount. . . . With limited resources, the United States must define the extent of its commitment and make a commitment commensurate with those realities. This may on occasion fall short of what some Americans would like and others would hope for." This vision of an America placing international leadership behind its own domestic economic objectives was soon denied by the administration, but seemed to many an accurate reflection of American policy. See Daniel Williams and John M. Goshko, "Reduced U.S. World Role Outlined but Soon Altered," *Washington Post*, May 26, 1993, pp. 1, 8.

[3] Figures for 1992 from International Institute for Strategic Studies (IISS), *The Military Balance, 1993-1994* (London: IISS/Brassey's, 1993).

Selected Bibliography

Adenauer, Konrad. *Erinnerungen: 1959-63.* Stuttgart: Deutsche Verlags-Anstalt, 1965.

Adrets, André (pseudonym). "Les relation franco-allemandes et le fait nucléaire dans une Europe divisée." *Politique étrangère* no. 3 (Fall 1984):649-664.

Alia, Josette and Christine Clerc. *La Guerre de Mitterrand: La dernière illusion.* Paris: Olivier Orbin, 1991.

Aron, Raymond. "Historical Sketch of the Great Debate." In Raymond Aron and Daniel Lerner, eds., *France Defeats the EDC.* New York: Frederick A. Praeger 1957.

Asmus, Ronald D. *Germany in Transition: National Self-Confidence and International Reticence.* N-3352-AF. Santa Monica, CA: RAND Corporation, 1992.

———. "Germany's Geopolitical Maturation: Strategy and Public Opinion After the Wall." *RAND Issue Paper.* (February 1993).

Axt, Heinz-Jürgen. "Hat Genscher Jugoslawien entzweit? Mythen und Fakten zur Aussenpolitik des vereinten Deutschlands." *Europa Archiv* 12 (1993):351-360.

Badinter Plan, text. In *Bulletin.* No. 144/S1173. Bonn: Presse und Informationsamt der Bundesregierung, December 19, 1991.

Barzel, Rainer. *25 Jahre deutsch-französische Zusammenarbeit/25ans de coopération franco-allemande.* Bonn: Bundesrepublik Deutschland, Presse- und Informationsamt der Bundesregierung (November 1987).

Bertram, Christoph. "Europe's Security Dilemmas." *Foreign Affairs* 65, no. 5 (Summer 1987):942-957.

Bozo, Frédéric. "Paradigm Lost: The French Experience with Détente." In Richard Davy, ed., *European Détente: A Reappraisal*. London: Royal Institute of International Affairs, 1991.

——. *La France et l'OTAN: De la guerre froide au nouvel ordre européen*. Paris: Masson, 1991.

Brenner, Michael and Phil Williams. *Europe and the United States: Security Policy Toward Europe in the 1990's*. Internal Studies no. 36. Sankt Augustin: Konrad Adenauer Stiftung, 1992.

Brubacker, Rogers. *Citizenship and Nationhood in France and Germany*. Cambridge, MA: Harvard University Press, 1992.

Buchheim, Hans. *Deutschlandpolitik, 1949-72: Der politischdiplomatische Prozess*. Stuttgart: Deutsche Verlags-Anstalt, 1984.

Colard, Daniel. "Convergences et Divergences politiques." *Documents* 2 (1974).

Calleo, David P. *Beyond American Hegemony: The Future of the Western Alliance*. New York: Basic Books, 1987.

Campbell, Edwina S. *Germany's Past & Europe's Future: The Challenges of West German Foreign Policy*. Washington DC: Pergamon/Brassy's, 1989.

Chirac, Jacques. "Contradictions et Convergences dans les relations franco-allemandes depuis la chute du mur de Berlin." Text provided by the office of Jacques Chirac.

Crawford, Beverly. *German Foreign Policy After the Cold War: The Decision to Recognize Croatia*. University of California Center for German and European Studies Working Paper 2.21 (August 1993).

Dannreuther, Roland. *The Gulf Conflict: A Political and Strategic Analysis*. Adelphi Paper no. 264. London: International Institute for Strategic Studies, 1992.

de Gaulle, Charles. *The Complete War Memoirs of Charles de Gaulle.* vol. 3, *Salvation: 1944-46.* New York: Simon and Schuster, 1960.

Delors, Jacques. "European Integration and Security." *Survival* 23, no. 2 (March-April 1991):99-109.

Denison, Andrew. "Amerika und das Eurokorps." *Europäische Sicherheit* (March 1993):123-126.

Donfried, Karen E. "The Franco-German Eurocorps: Implications for the U.S. Security Role in Europe." (Washington DC: Congressional Research Service Report for Congress, 1992).

Dregger, Alfred. "Entwurf einer Sicherheitspolitik zur Selbstbehauptung Europas." *Europäische Wehrkünde* no. 12 (December 1987):303-312.

Enders, Thomas and Michael J. Inacker. "The Second Gulf War and Germany: Contributions and Political and Military Lessons." Unpublished paper presented to the Center for National Security Studies' study of foreign perspectives on the Gulf War, provided by Center for National Security Studies, Los Alamos National Laboratory, (October 1991).

Engels, Anne. "Die USA und der Europäische Pfeiler 1984-92: WEU und deutsch-französische Sicherheitskooperation aus amerikanischer Sicht." Unpublished master's thesis. Bonn University (1993).

European Union. "Security Policy Cooperation Within the Framework of the Common Foreign and Security Policy of the Political Union." *Europe Documents* series. Brussels: Agence International d'Information pour la Presse, February 21, 1991.

Fawcett, Louise and Robert O'Neill. "Britain, the Gulf Crisis and European Security." In Nicole Gnesotto and John Roper, eds., *Western Europe and the Gulf.* Paris: Institute for Security Studies, Western European Union, 1992.

Foreign Policy Institute. *The Franco-German Corps and the Future of European Security: Implications for U.S. Policy.* Washington DC: Foreign Policy Institute Policy Consensus Report, 1992.

France. Ministère des Affaires étrangères. *Bulletin d'information du ministère des Affaires étrangères* (series). Paris: Ministère des Affaires étrangères.

France. Ministère de la Défense. *Livre Blanc sur la Défense, 1994.* Paris: Service d'Information et de Relations Publiques des Armées, Ministère de la Défense, 1994.

France. Ministère des Relations Extérieures. *La politique étrangère de la France: Textes et documents* (series). Paris: Documentation Française.

France and Germany. "Summit of the Franco-German Defense and Security Council on May 22, 1991 in La Rochelle." Press release. Washington DC: Embassy of the Federal Republic of Germany, 1992.

Friend, Julius W. *The Linchpin: French-German Relations, 1950-1990.* The Washington Papers, no. 154. Washington DC: Praeger/Center for Strategic and International Studies, 1991.

Fursdon, Edward. *The EDC: A History.* London: Macmillan, 1980.

"Gansel-Bericht fordert Anerkennung Sloweniens und Kroatiens; Föderation souveräner Staaten vorgeschlagen." *Archiv der Gegenwart* no. 14 (June 28-July 7, 1991):35795-35797.

Garrity, Patrick J. *Why the Gulf War Still Matters: Foreign Perspectives on the War and the Future of International Security.* Report no. 16. Los Alamos, Center for National Security Studies, 1993.

Gebhard, Paul R.S. *The United States and European Security.* Adelphi Paper no. 286. London: International Institute for Strategic Studies, 1994.

Genscher, Hans-Dietrich. "Für Recht auf Selfstbestimmung." *Das Parlament.* (November 15/22, 1991).

———. *Wir wollen ein Europäisches Deutschland.* Berlin: Goldman, 1991.

German Information Center. "German Support for the Transition to Democracy and Market Economy in the Former Soviet Union." New York: German Information Service, 1992.

——. "Kinkel Appeals to Serbian Leadership to 'Stop Murder and Destruction.'" *This Week in Germany*. New York: German Information Center, June 12, 1992.

Germany. *Weißbuch 1994 zur Sicherheit der Bundesrepublik Deutschland und zur Lage und Zukunft der Bundeswehr.* Bonn: Federal Ministry of Defence, 1994.

Glenny, Misha. *The Fall of Yugoslavia: The Third Balkan War*. New York: Penguin Books, 1992.

——. "Hope for Bosnia?" *New York Review of Books* (April 7, 1994): 6-8.

Gnesotto, Nicole and John Roper, eds. *Western Europe and the Gulf.* Paris: Institute for Security Studies, Western European Union, 1992.

Gordon, Philip H. *A Certain Idea of France: French Security Policy and the Gaullist Legacy.* Princeton, NJ: Princeton University Press, 1993.

——. *Die Deutsch-Französische Partnerschaft und die Atlantische Allianz.* Arbeitspapiere zur Internationalen Politik 82. Bonn: Forschungsinstitut der Deutschen Gesellschaft für Auswärtige Politik, 1994.

——. *French Security Policy after the Cold War: Continuity, Change and Implications for the United States.* R-4229-A. Santa Monica, CA: RAND Corporation, 1992.

——. "The Normalization of German Foreign Policy." *Orbis* 38, no. 2 (Spring 1994):225-243.

Grant, Robert P., *The Changing Franco-American Security Relationship: New Directions for NATO and European Defense Cooperation.* Arlington, VA: U.S.-CREST, December 1993.

Grosser, Alfred. *La IVᵉ République et sa politique extérieure.* Paris: Armand Colin, 1961.

Guérin-Sendelbach, Valérie. *Ein Tandem für Europa? Die Deutsch-Französische Zusammenarbeit der achtziger Jahre.* Arbeitspapiere zur Internationalen Politik 77. Bonn: Forschungsinstitut der Deutschen Gesellschaft für Auswärtige Politik, 1993.

Guicherd, Catherine. *L'heure de l'Europe: premières leçons du conflit yougoslave.* Paris: Les Cahiers du Crest, 1993.

Haglund, David. *Alliance Within the Alliance?: Franco-German Military Cooperation and the European Pillar of Defense.* Boulder, CO: Westview, 1991.

Hahn, Walter F. "West Germany's Ostpolitik: The Grand Design of Egon Bahr." *Orbis* (Winter 1973).

Hanrieder, Wolfram F. *Germany, America, Europe: Forty Years of German Foreign Policy.* New Haven: Yale University, 1989.

Harris, Scott A. and James B. Steinberg. *European Defense and the Future of Transatlantic Relations.* MR-276. Santa Monica, CA: RAND Corporation, 1993.

Harrison, Michael M. *The Reluctant Ally: France and Atlantic Security.* Baltimore: The Johns Hopkins University Press, 1981.

Heisbourg, François. "France and the Gulf Crisis." In Nicole Gnesotto and John Roper, eds., *Western Europe and the Gulf.* Paris: Institute for Security Studies, Western European Union, 1992.

Hernu, Charles. "Face à la logique des blocs, une France indépendante et solidaire." *Défense nationale* (December 1982).

Hoffmann, Stanley. *Decline or Renewal? France Since the 1930's.* New York: The Viking Press, 1974.

———. "La France dans le nouvel ordre européen." *Politique étrangère* (Fall 1990).

Inotai, Andras. "Economic Implications of German Unification for Central and Eastern Europe." In Paul B. Stares, ed., *The New Germany and the New Europe.* Washington DC: The Brookings Institution, 1992.

International Institute for Strategic Studies (IISS). *The Military Balance* (annual series). London: IISS/Brassey's, 1993.

International Monetary Fund (IMF). *Direction of Trade Statistics Yearbook.* Washington DC: IMF, 1993.

Joffe, Josef. "The New Europe: Yesterday's Ghosts." *Foreign Affairs* 72, no. 1 (America and the World, 1992/92).

Joxe, Pierre. "Discours d'ouverture." In *Un nouveau débat stratégique.* Actes du colloque de Paris, 1992.

Kaiser, Karl and Klaus Becher. *Deutschland und der Irak-Konflikt: Internationale Sicherheitsverantwortung Deutschlands und Europas nach der deutschen Vereinigung.* Arbeitspapiere zur Internationalen Politik 68. Bonn: Forschungsinstitut der Deutschen Gesellschaft für Auswärtige Politik, 1992.

Kaiser, Karl and Pierre Lellouche. *Deutsch-französische Sicherheitspolitik.* Bonn: Europa Verlag, Forschungsinstitut der Deutschen Gesellschaft für Auswärtige Politik, 1986. Published in French as *Le couple franco-allemand et la défense de l'Europe.* Paris: Institut Français des Relations Internationales, 1986.

Kelleher, Catherine McArdle. *Germany and the Politics of Nuclear Weapons.* New York: Columbia University Press, 1975.

Keohane, Robert O. *Neorealism and its Critics.* New York: Columbia University Press, 1986.

Keohane, Robert O., Joseph S. Nye, and Stanley Hoffmann. *After the Cold War: International Institutions and State Strategies in Europe, 1989-1991.* Cambridge, MA: Harvard University Press, 1993.

Klein, Jean. "Mythes et réalités de la défense de l'Europe." *Politique étrangère* 2 (1983).

Kohl, Wilfred L. *French Nuclear Diplomacy.* Princeton, NJ: Princeton University Press, 1971.

Kolboom, Ingo. *Vom geteilten zum vereinten Deutschland: Deutschland-Bilder in Frankreich.* Arbeitspapiere zur Internationalen Politik 61. Bonn: Forschungsinstitut der Deutschen Gesellschaft für Auswärtige Politik, 1991.

Kolodziej, Edward. *French International Policy Under de Gaulle and Pompidou: The Politics of Grandeur.* Ithaca: Cornell University Press, 1974.

Lacouture, Jean. *De Gaulle*. vol. 3, *Le Souverain, 1959-70*. Paris: Le Seuil, 1986.

Lamers, Karl. "Eine Sicherheits-Union--Möglichkeiten und Grenzen: Zu Einer deutsch-französischen Parlamentarier Initiative." *Dokumente* 47 (February 1991):17-22.

Le Gloannec, Anne-Marie. "The Implications of German Unification for Western Europe." In Paul B. Stares, ed., *The New Germany and the New Europe*. Washington DC: The Brookings Institution, 1992.

Lellouche, Pierre. "France in Search of Security." *Foreign Affairs* 72, no. 2 (Spring 1993):121-131.

——. *Le nouveau monde: De l'ordre de Yalta au désordre des nations*. Paris: Grasset, 1992.

Livingston, Robert Gerald. "United Germany: Bigger and Better." *Foreign Policy* no. 87 (Summer 1992).

McCarthy, Patrick. *France-Germany, 1983-93: The Struggle to Cooperate*. New York, St. Martin's Press, 1993.

McGeehan, Robert. *The German Rearmament Question: American Diplomacy and European Defense after World War II*. Urbana, IL: University of Illinois Press, 1971.

Maillard, Pierre. *De Gaulle et l'Allemagne: Le rêve inachevé*. Paris: Plon, 1990.

Markovits, Andrei S. and Simon Reich. *The New Face of Germany: Gramsci, Neorealism and Hegemony*. Center for European Studies Working Paper Series no. 28. Cambridge: Harvard University Press, no date.

Maull, Hanns W. "Germany's New Foreign Policy." In Hanns W. Maull and Philip H. Gordon, *German Foreign Policy and the German `National Interest': German and American Perspectives*. Seminar Papers no. 5. Washington DC: American Institute for Contemporary German Studies, 1993.

Mearsheimer, John J. "Back to the Future: Instability in Europe after the Cold War." *International Security* 15, no. 1 (Summer 1990):5-56.

——. "Why We Will Soon Miss the Cold War." *Atlantic Monthly* 66 (August 1990).

Méry, General Guy. "Comments by General Guy Méry, March 15, 1976." *Survival* 118, no. 5 (September-October 1976):226-228.

——. "Une armée pour quoi faire et comment?" *Défense nationale* 32 (June 1976):11-24.

Millotat, Christian and Jean-Claude Philippot. "Le jumelage franco-allemand pour la sécurité de l'Europe." *Défense nationale* (October 1990).

Minc, Alain. *La Grande Illusion.* Paris: Grasset, 1989.

Mitterrand, François. Interview with Jean Daniel. *Nouvel Observateur* (December 18-24, 1987).

——. "Press Conference of François Mitterrand, President of the Republic of France, March 7, 1986." *Survival* no. 4 (1986).

——. *Réflexions sur la politique extérieure de la France.* Paris: Fayard, 1986.

Mühlen, Alexander. "Die deutsch Rolle bei der Anerkennung der jugoslawischen Sezessionsstaaten." *Liberal* no. 2 (June 1992).

Müller, Harald. "German Foreign Policy After Unification." In Paul B. Stares, ed., *The New Germany and the New Europe.* Washington DC: The Brookings Institution, 1992.

Newhouse, John. "The Diplomatic Round: Dodging the Problem." *The New Yorker* (August 24, 1992):60-71.

North Atlantic Treaty Organization. *NATO: Facts about the North Atlantic Treaty Organization.* Paris: NATO Information Service, 1965.

O'Brien, Conor Cruise. "The Future of the West." *The National Interest* (Winter 1992-93):3-10.

Organization for Economic Co-operation and Development. *Development Co-operation.* Paris: OECD, 1994.

Picht, Robert, ed. *Das Bündnis im Bündnis: Deutsch-französiche Beziehungen im internationalen Spannungsfeld.* Berlin: Severin und Siedler, 1982.

Poidevin, Raymond. "Der Faktor Europas in der Deutschlandpolitik Robert Schumans 1948/49." *Vierteljahreshefte für Zeitgeschichte* (July 1985).

Rioux, Jean-Pierre. *La France de la Quatrième République: L'ardeur et la nécessité, 1944-1952.* Paris: Editions du Seuil, 1980.

Rocard, Michel. *Europe and the United States.* Critical Issues no. 2. Leffingwell Lecture Series at the Council on Foreign Relations in New York. New York: Council on Foreign Relations Press, 1992.

Rühe, Volker. "Shaping Euro-Atlantic Policies: A Grand Strategy for a New Era." *Survival* 3, no. 2 (Summer 1993):129-137.

Schlör, Wolfgang. *German Security Policy.* Adelphi Paper no. 264. London: International Institute for Stratgic Studies, 1993.

Schmidt, Helmut. "Deutsch-französische Zusammenarbeit in der Sicherheitspolitik." *Europa-Archiv* no. 11 (1987):303-312.

———. *Die Deutschen und ihre Nachbarn.* Berlin: Goldman, 1990.

Schmidt, Peter. "The Franco-German Defense and Security Council." *Aussenpolitik* (English edition) 40, no. 4 (1989):360-371.

———. *The Special Franco-German Security Relationship in the 1990's.* Chaillot Paper no. 8. Paris: WEU Institute for Security Studies, 1993.

Schwarz, Hans-Peter. *Adenauer: Der Aufstieg, 1876-1952.* Stuttgart: Deutsche Verlags-Anstalt, 1986.

———. *Eine Entente Elémentaire.* Arbeitspapiere zur Internationalen Politik 47. Bonn: Forschungsinstitut der Deutschen Gesellschaft für Auswärtig Politik, 1990.

Soros, George. "Prospects for European Disintegration." Speech delivered to the Aspen Institute Berlin, September 29, 1993. New York: Soros Foundation, 1993.

Soutou, Georges-Henri. "Die Nuklearpolitik der vierten Republik." *Vierteljahreshefte für Zeitgeschichte* (October 1989).

Stark, Hans. "Dissonances franco-allemandes sur fond de guerre serbo-croate." *Politique étrangère* 2 (1992).

Steininger, Rolf. "Das Scheitern der EVG und der Beitritt der Bundesrepublik zur NATO." *Aus Politik und Zeitgeschichte,* supplement to *Das Parlament* B17/8 (1985):3-18.

Steinberg, James B. *"An Ever Closer Union": European Integration and its Implications for the Future of U.S.-European Relations.* R-4177-A. Santa Monica, CA: RAND Corporation, 1993.

———. *The Role of European Institutions in Security After the Cold War: Some Lessons from Yugoslavia.* N-3445-FF. Santa Monica, CA: RAND Corporation, 1992.

Szabo, Steven F. *The Changing Politics of German Security.* London: Pinter, 1990.

———. *The Diplomacy of German Unification.* New York: St. Martin's Press, 1993.

Taft, William H. IV. "Die Europäische Sicherheit und die Lehren aus dem Golfkrieg". *NATO-Brief* 39, no.3 (1991).

Touchard, Jean. *Le gaullisme: 1940-1969.* Paris: Editions du Seuil, 1987.

Valence, Georges. *France-Allemagne: Le Retour de Bismarck.* Paris: Flammarion, 1990.

Walt, Stephen M. "Alliances: Balancing and Bandwagoning." In Robert J. Art and Robert Jervis, eds., *International Politics: Enduring Concepts and Contemporary Issues.* 3rd edition. (New York: Harper Collins Publishers, 1992), pp. 70-78.

Waltz, Kenneth N. *Theory of International Politics.* Reading, MA: Addison-Wesley, 1979.

Western European Union. "Declaration of the Member States of Western European Union which are also members of the European Union on the role of WEU and its relations with the European Union and with the Atlantic Alliance." Western European Union, December 10, 1991.

Willis, Roy F. *France, Germany and the New Europe: 1945-67*. Rev. ed. New York: Oxford University Press, 1968.

Yost, David S. "France in the New Europe." *Foreign Affairs* 69, no. 5 (Winter 1990-91):107-128.

——. "France and the Persian Gulf War of 1990-1991: Political-Military Lessons Learned." *Journal of Strategic Studies* 16, no. 3 (September 1993).

——. "France and West European Defence Identity." *Survival* 33, no. 4 (July-August 1991):327-351.

——. "Franco-German Defence Cooperation." In Stephen F. Szabo, ed., *The Bundeswehr and Western Security*. New York: St. Martin's Press, 1990.

Index

Adenauer, Konrad, i, 12-14, 25n.9, 26n.12, 27n.17, 40, 93
Afghanistan: Soviet invasion of, 17
Africa, 33, 87
AlphaJet squadron, 37
Arms control and disarmament negotiations, 17, 22, 23
Asylum seekers, 47, 56
Atlantic Alliance, ii, iii, 9, 16, 18, 21, 38, 39, 42, 44, 51, 83, 85, 102-104
Atlanticism, 14-17, 38, 40, 83; and Europeanism, 40, 41
Austria, 52
AWACS, 62, 90

Bahr, Egon, 16, 27n.20
Baker, James, 42, 70n.3
Balkans, see Yugoslavia
Balladur, Edouard, 49, 50, 73n.57, 87, 88, 95n.7, 96n.27, 98n.48; government of, 96n.28
Balladur Plan, 50
Barre, Raymond, 17
Baumel, Jacques, 84
Belgium: and Eurocorps, 41, 43, 105; and Gulf War, 37
Biden, Joseph, 81n.120
Blair House accords, 92
Bold Sparrow (operation), 20, 21
Bosnia, 59-64, 78n.101, 85, 87, 90
Bosnian Moslems, 57, 60, 62-64; and UN arms embargo, 63
Bourgès-Manoury, Maurice, 13
Brandt, Willy, 15, 16
Bujon de l'Estang, François, 84, 88

Bush, George, 32, 97n.33; and Eurocorps, 42; and Germany, 38

Cambodia, 87; UN in, 90
Canadian battalion in former Yugoslavia, 64
Carter, Jimmy, 16
Central Europe, 47-53, 56, 72n.45, 72n.50, 101, 105
Central Asia, 50
Chaban-Delmas, Jacques, 13
Cheney, Dick, 42
Chevènement, Jean-Pierre, 35
Chirac, Jacques, 17, 29n.40, 88; and Iraq, 35; and NATO, 84; and nuclear weapons, 22
Christian Democratic Union (CDU), 39, 55, 91, 92
Christian Social Union (CSU), 55
Christopher, Warren 60, 63, 78n.105, 80n.118
Clinton, Bill, 32; and domestic politics, 106; and Partnership for Peace, 51; and war in former Yugoslavia, 63
Common Agricultural Policy (CAP), 93
Common Foreign and Security Policy (CFSP), ii, 38-40, 50, 65, 68n.18, 105
Conference on Security and Cooperation in Europe (CSCE), 48, 84, 93n.3
Corsica, 57

Croatia: peacekeeping in, 85;
   recognition of, 52-58, 60, 75n.77,
   75n.79, 76n.83-4, 77n.94,
   78n.105, 102; and splitting of
   Bosnia, 64; UN buffer force in,
   63; Ustasha, 59
Czech Republic, 47, 49

de Gaulle, Charles, i, 10, 12-15, 22,
   24n.3, 25n.7, 27n.16, 27n.18, 40
Decoupling, 18, 20
Delors, Jacques, 39, 68n.16
Detente: and France, 14; and
   Germany, 14, 22, 23
Dumas, Roland, 39, 42, 58-60,
   75n.79, 77n.95, 84, 87

East Berlin, Mitterrand in, 87
East Germany (GDR): and
   Ostpolitik, 15, 16, 21; and West
   Germany, 46
Eastern Europe, ii, 15, 19, 20, 33,
   34, 36, 46-3, 56-58, 101, 105,
   106; defined, 72n.45; revolutions
   in 1989, 36; Soviet occupation of,
   32
El Salvador, 87
Elysée Treaty, i, 13, 14, 18, 26n.15,
   27n.17, 41, 53, 68n.21, 107;
   Bundestag preamble to, 14,
   27n.17; twenty-fifth anniversary
   of, 23, 26n.15
Erhard, Ludwig, 14, 15
Ethnic cleansing, 63
Eurocorps, ii, 41-46, 68n.20, 70n.32,
   71n.39, 71n.43, 90, 92, 104, 105,
   107; and NATO, 42-43
European Central Bank, 93
European Coal and Steel Community
   (ECSC), 12, 105
European Community, i, 13, 19, 47,
   106; and Atlantic Alliance, iii;
   Common Agricultural Policy of,
93; Commission of, 39; Common
   foreign and security policy of, ii,
   38-40, 50, 65, 105; Council of,
   50; and Eastern Europe, 48-50;
   and economic union, 104;
   enlargement of, 51, 105; and
   European pillar, 42; and European
   security identity, 39, 40, 43, 46,
   84, 85, 90, 103; and France, 58;
   and Gulf war, 38, 39; and
   Maastricht, 41, 88, 105; and
   NATO, 41; and Ostpolitik, 52;
   and monetary union, 54, 88; and
   single market, 102; and UK, 14;
   and US, 38; and WEU, 41, 61;
   and war in former Yugoslavia, 53,
   54, 60, 62, 64-66
European Defence Community
   (EDC), 12, 13, 25n.9-10, 26n.11
European Economic Community
   (EEC), see European Community
European Monetary System, 15, 16,
   105; exchange rate mechanism
   (ERM), 89
European Monetary Union (EMU),
   54, 88
European Parliament, 39
European Union (EU), see European
   Community

Fabius, Laurent, 60
Federal Democratic Party (FDP), 91-
   93
Federalism, 88
Force Action Rapide (FAR), 19, 20
Fouchet Plan, 41
France: and arms control, 17; and
   Central and Eastern Europe, 47-
   50, 52, 53, 57; economy of, 17;
   and Gulf war, 3, 24n.5, 37-40, 87,
   94n.6; and military, 16, 19, 20,
   23, 37, 61, 87; and military
   doctrine, 16; and military

independence, 10, 14, 16, 17, 21, 36, 84, 86; and military spending, 16, 96n.21; and NATO, iii, 10, 14, 17, 19, 21, 27n.16, 27n.23, 31, 43-45, 49, 51, 58, 61, 62, 83-86, 94n.6, 95n.10, 95n.12-13, 101; nuclear force of, 10, 11, 13, 14, 16, 18, 20, 22-23, 27n.24, 29n.36, 31, 33, 46, 86, 97n.32; and reconciliation with Germany, 13, 14, 24, 31, 32; and status (grandeur, prestige, rank), 9, 10, 21, 24n.3, 35, 36, 66n.6, 67n.7, 87; and war in former Yugoslavia, 54, 57-63, 65, 77n.95, 79n.106

France-Iraq Friendship Society, 35

Franco-German brigade, 23, 24, 34, 41, 43

French Socialist Party (PS): and Eastern Europe, 49; and German Socialists, 17, 18; and German unification, 87, 88; and Iraq, 35; and NATO, 84

Fuchs, Gérard, 39

Galvin, John, 42, 43

Gaullism, 9, 10, 15

Genscher, Hans-Dietrich: and Euromissiles, 23; and Gorbachev, 22, 29n.38; and Gulf war, 39; and recognition of Croatia and Slovenia, 53, 55, 56, 77n.89

German Green Party, 21

German Socialist Party (SPD): and Eurocorps, 42, 69n.24; and France, 21; and French Socialists, 17, 18; and peacekeeping, 91, 92, 98n.45; and war in former Yugoslavia, 55, 62, 76n.84

Germany: Bundeswehr, 23, 27n.8; and Central and Eastern Europe, 47-53, 55, 56, 58, 7n.49-50, 93, 106; and currency union, 36; and

Eurocorps, 71n.39, 71n.43, fears about, iii, 87-89; and Gulf War, 25n.5, 36-40, 90; and NATO, iii, 12, 15, 17, 18, 21, 42, 43, 51, 62, 67n.8, 89-91, 101; and nuclear weapons, 10, 11, 13, 14, 20, 26n.13, 27n.16, 90; and rearmament, 12,13; reconcilation with France, 13, 14, 24, 31, 32; relations with US, iii, 17, 18, 21, 31, 37, 42, 43, 61, 70,n.35, 89, 90, 92, 97n.33; and Soviet Union, 29n.39; troop deployments of, 91; and UN Security Council, 90, 93; unification, ii, 33, 34, 36, 46, 55, 56, 58, 61, 83, 87, 90, 92, 97n.33, 103; and war in former Yugoslavia, 37, 53-63, 65, 77n.91, 90; and WEU, 26n.12

Giraud, André, 20

Giscard d'Estaing, Valéry, 10, 15-17, 28n.25-26, 88

Gorbachev, Mikhail, 22

Great Britain: 10, 14, 36-40, 45, 62, 63, 65, 88, 93; and Eurocorps, 41; and France, 15, 104; and Gulf war, 37, 38, 67n.12; military expenditure of, 107; and NATO, 68n.18; "special relationship" with US, 38, 39; and war in former Yugoslavia, 54, 59, 60

Greece, 105

Gulf war, see Persian Gulf war

Hawk missiles, 37

Helsinki Final Act, 50

Hernu, Charles, 19

Hoffmann, Stanley, 33, 73n.53

Hurd, Douglas, 59, 68n.18, 78n.99

Hussein, Saddam, 35, 37

INF treaty, 20, 22

Intermediate-range nuclear force (INF), 17, 18, 20, 22

Iran, 90
Iraq, 25n.5, 34, 36; and France, 35, 87; sanctions against, 37
Islamic fundamentalism, 33
Italy, 13; and Eurocorps, 41

Jobert, Michel, 15
Joxe, Pierre, 84
Juppé, Alain, 78n.97, 84

Kennedy, John F., 22, 40
Kiev, Mitterrand in, 87
Kimmit, Robert, 42
Kinkel, Klaus: and Eastern Europe, 51, 74n.64; and Eurocorps, 70n.35, 90; and France, 93; and war in former Yugoslavia, 61, 78n.105, 79n.111
Kohl, Helmut, 18, 23, 79n.111, 98n.48; and Eastern Europe, 49; and Eurocorps, 42; and Franco-German brigade, 41; and Iraq, 36; and military forces, 90, 91, and Mitterrand, 19, 20, 23, 41, 71n.39; and Polish border, 52; and trade, 92; and UN Security Council, 90; and war in former Yugoslavia, 54, 80n.116; and World War II, 93
Kohl-Mitterrand proposal, 41, 68n.17, 68n.20
Korean War, 12
Kurds, 90
Kuwait, 25n.5, 35, 36, 87

La Rochelle summit, 42, 43, 70n.35, 71n.38
Lambsdorff, Otto Graf, 93, 80n.111
Lamers, Karl, 393, 51
Lanxade, Jacques, 44
Lellouche, Pierre, 84, 88
Léotard, François, 49, 51, 85

Luns, Joseph, 40
Luxembourg, and Eurocorps, 41

Maastricht summit (December 1991), 41
Maastricht treaty, 68n.19, 69n.23, 88, 105
Macedonia, 59
Macmillan, Harold, 40
Major, John, 38
Méry, Guy, 16, 27n.24, 28n.25
Middle East: and France, 36; peace process, 104, 105
Mitterrand, François, 10; and Bundestag speech, 18-19, 28n.30; and Commmon Foreign and Security Policy, 50; and detente, 22; and Eastern Europe, 48, 49, 57, 72n.52, 73n.53; and German unification, 87; and Gulf War, 35, 36, 67n.9; and Kohl, 18, 20, 23, 41, 71n.39; and nuclear policy, 18, 23, 29n.36, 29n.40-41, 87, 97n.32; and recognition of Croatia and Slovenia, 60; and Serbia, 58, 59; and Soviet Union, 18; and US, 28n.34, 71n.38; and war in former Yugoslavia, 78n.102, 79n.110, 87
Montenegro, 61
Moscow, Jobert in, 15

NATO, see North Atlantic Treaty Organization
NATO Defence Planning Committee (DPC), 85, 86
NATO Military Committee, 85
NATO Nuclear Planning Group, 85
NATO Rapid Raction Corps, 90, 103
NATO summit (December 1993), 50-52
NATO summit (January 1994), 64, 85

Naumann, Klaus, 43
Netherlands: and Eurocorps, 41; and Gulf war, 38; and WEU, 40
North Atlantic Treaty Organization (NATO), i, 13, 38; and Allied Command Europe Mobile Force, 37; and article 5, 43, 45; and Balladur, 49; and Defence Planning Committee, 85, 86; and de Gaulle 14; and Eastern Europe, 49-51; and Eurocorps, 41-44, 70n.35; European caucus of, 46; and EC, 40, 41, 43; and France, iii, 10, 14, 17, 19, 21, 27n.16, 27n.23, 31, 43-45, 49-51, 58, 61, 62, 83-86, 94n.6, 95n.10, 95n.12-13, 101; and Germany, iii, 12, 15, 17, 18, 19, 21, 42, 43, 51, 62, 89-91, 101; January 1994 summit, 50, 64, 85; and Kohl, 18, 23, 36; March 1988 summit, 23; and Military Committee, 85; and Mitterrand, 23; and NAC, 86; and nuclear deterrence, 17; and Nuclear Planning Group, 85; and out-of-area issue, 36, 90; and Partnership for Peace, 57; peacekeepers, 51; Rapid Reaction Corps of, 102; and US, 38, 42, 46, 51, 86; and war in former Yugoslavia, 63-64, 83-86; and WEU, 41, 68n.19
North Africa, 33, 35, 48, 105, 106
North Atlantic Cooperation Council (NACC), 49-51, 73n.56, 90
Northern Ireland, 59
Nuclear weapons: European nuclear cooperation, 13, 106; and France, 10, 11, 13, 14, 18, 22, 35, 36, 61, 63, 65, 86, 90, 93; Franco-German nuclear program, 13, 14, 26n.13, 27n.16; and Germany, 10, 11, 13, 14, 16, 17, 20, 22, 26n.13,

90; INF treaty, 20, 22; proliferation of, 33; short range, 23; and US, 31

Oil crisis, 17
Ostpolitik, 14-16, 21, 27n.20, 46, 51, 58

Parti Socialist, see French Socialist Party
Partnership for Peace, 51
Peacekeeping: and Eurocorps, 43-45; and EC, 106; and France, 84; and Germany, 91, 92; and NATO, 51, 86; and war in former Yugoslavia, 62-64
Pershing missile (Euromissile) deployments, 18, 19, 22
Persian Gulf War, ii, 24n.5, 35-40, 45, 59, 65, 84, 90, 91, 94n.6, 101, 103, 104
Pleven Plan, 12
Pleven, René, 12
Poland: border with Germany, 47, 52; and EC, 105; and ethnic Germans, 47; and Ostpolitik, 15; and Partnership for Peace, 51; and Soviet Union, 17; and trade, 74n.74
Pompidou, Georges, 15, 27n.21
Portugal, 105
Powell, Colin, 42

Rally for the Republic (RPR), 49, 84, 88
Rambouillet, meeting of de Gaulle and Adenauer, 13
Reagan, Ronald, 20, 27n.17
Red Army, 11
Refugees, 47, 56
Reykjavik summit, 20
Rocard, Michel, 71n.38

Rognoni, Verginio, 41
Roland missiles, 37
Roman Catholic Church, and
  Germany, 55, 60, 76n.82
Russia, 34; and ethnic Germans, 47;
  and European confederation, 48;
  and France, 48, 83; and US, 104;
  and war in former Yugoslavia, 62
Rühe, Volker, 51, 55, 61

Sarajevo, 62, 64, 87; German airlifts
  to, 87; market massacre, 64
Saudi Arabia, 37
Scandinavia, and EU entry, 52
Schmidt, Helmut, 18; and Giscard,
  15-17, 28n.26
Scowcroft, Brent, 42
Serbia, 55-64, 90
Shalikashvili, John, 43
Slovenia, recognition of, 53-58, 60,
  75n.77, 75n.79, 76n.83-84,
  77n.94, 78n.105, 102
Somalia, 45; and France 87; and
  Germany, 90; and US, 104
South America, 87
South Pacific, 87
South Lebanon, 87
Southern Europe, 33
Soviet Union: ii, 11, 32, 34, 104; and
  Afghanistan, 17; aid to, 105; and
  Balkans, 59; and Central Europe,
  48; and detente, 14, 15; and
  ethnic Germans, 47; and France,
  18, 46, 49, 57; and Germany, 18,
  22, 49; and two-plus-four
  agreements, 37; and US, 33
Soviet threat, ii, 9, 22, 32, 34, 40, 91
Spaak, Paul-Henri, 40
Spain: and war in former Yugoslavia,
  62; and Eurocorps, 41, 69n.22
Special relationship (US and UK),
  38, 39

Srebrenica, 64
Strasbourg, 43, 45
Strategic Defence Initiative (SDI), 20
Strauss, Franz-Josef, 13, 26n.13
Supreme Allied Commander Europe
  (SACEUR), 21, 42-44, 86
Sweden, 105
Syria, 87

Taft, William IV, 38, 42
Treaty of Rome, 13
Turkey, 37
Two-plus-four treaty (Germany), 37

Ukraine, 47
Union for French Democracy (UDF),
  84, 88
United Kingdom, see Great Britain
United Nations, (UN): and borders,
  50; and Cambodia, 90; and France,
  61, 84, 87; and Germany, 90-92;
  and Gulf war, 35, 39; Security
  Council, 9, 10, 35, 36, 61, 63, 65,
  86, 90, 93; and war in former
  Yugoslavia, 60, 61
United Nations (UN) Security
  Council, 9, 10, 35, 36, 61, 63, 65,
  86, 90, 93
United States: 40, 44, 51, 91, 92, 107;
  and defence of Europe, i, ii, 11, 16,
  18, 20, 32, 33, 105-107, 108n.2;
  domestic politics, 32; and
  Eurocorps, 42, 69n.25; and Gulf
  war, 37-40, 44, 45, 67n.14, 103;
  and NATO, 38, 42, 46, 51, 86; and
  nuclear weapons, 31; and
  Ostpolitik, 16; relations with
  France, 23, 36, 48, 50, 71n.38, 83-
  86, 88-90, 92; relations with
  Germany, iii, 12, 15, 17, 18, 21,
  31, 37, 42, 43, 61, 89, 90, 92,
  97n.33; relations with Soviet
  Union, 20, 33; and "special

relationship" with UK, 38, 39;
and war in former Yugoslavia, 53,
59, 60, 63-66, 71n.38, 80n.119,
104
US Congress, 42
Ustasha, 59

Van den Broek, Hans, 41
Vance, Cyrus, 60
Vance-Owen Peace Plan
(Yugoslavia), 85
Verheugen, Günter, 92
Vietnam, US lessons of, 59

Waigel, Theo, 93
Warsaw Pact, 33, 46
Washington Plan (for Bosnia), 62
Wehrmacht, 91
Weizsäcker, Richard von, 22
Western Sahara, 87
Western European Union (WEU), 40,
68n.20-21, 69n.21; and Eastern
Europe, 50, 51; and EC, 41; and
France, 61, 62, 85; and Germany,
12, 15, 26n.12; and NATO, 13,
43, 61, 68n.19; relaunching of,
15, 19, 28n.31
White Paper 1994 (France), 74n.72,
85-87, 95n.12
White Paper 1994 (Germany), 91
World War II, 9, 10, 36, 59, 91, 92,
98n.41

Yalta, 49
Yost, David, 46
Yugoslavia, war in, ii, 37, 45, 50, 53-
65, 81n.124, 85, 87, 101-103,
105, 106; and arms embargo, 63;
and naval embargo, 61; and no-
fly-zone, 61, 62, 85; and self-
determination, 60; and
Washington Plan, 62

Zhirinovsky, Vladimir, 50

About the Book
and Author

Examining the Franco-German security partnership in its post–Cold War context, Philip Gordon analyzes the implications of that partnership for both Europe and the United States. Utilizing French and German sources and extensive interviews in Paris, Bonn, and Washington, the author traces the evolution of Franco-German security cooperation since World War II, focusing especially on the post-1989 period. Detailed case studies of the Persian Gulf War, the debates over the "Eurocorps," policies toward Eastern Europe, and the war in Yugoslavia make an invaluable contribution to our understanding of French, German, and Alliance policies in the post–Cold War world. Gordon identifies new trends in French and German security policies since 1989, concluding that the general commitment in Paris and Berlin to continued cooperation is not in doubt but that a truly common and effective Franco-German or European security policy is unlikely.

Philip H. Gordon is Carol Deane Senior Fellow in U.S. Strategic Studies and editor of *Survival* at the International Institute for Strategic Studies in London. He is also the author of *A Certain Idea of France: French Security Policy and the Gaullist Legacy.*